ROBIN WARD'S **VAN COU VER**

ROBIN WARD'S

VAN COU VER

HARBOUR PUBLISHING

Harbour Publishing Co. Ltd.
Box 219, Madeira Park BC
Canada V0N 2H0

Copyright © 1990 by Robin Ward

Designed by Robin Ward
Edited by Mary Schendlinger
Typeset in Gill Sans
Printed and bound in Canada by Friesen Printers

Canadian Cataloguing in Publication Data

Ward, Robin, 1950–
Robin Ward's Vancouver

ISBN 1-55017-030-9

1. Historic buildings—British Columbia—
Vancouver—Pictorial works.   2. Vancouver (B.C.)—
Buildings, structures, etc.—Pictorial works.
3. Vancouver (B.C.)—History—Pictorial works.
   FC3847.7.W37 1990   971.1'33'00222
   F1089.5.V22W37 1990   C90-091597-8

CONTENTS

When I first began drawing and writing about Vancouver's architectural heritage for the *Vancouver Sun*, one of the editors on the paper exclaimed, "Are you sure there's enough? Look at it!" He waved his arm at the glistening, modern skyline across False Creek. "Where's the heritage? They're knocking it down." From a distance, Vancouver does look like a brash parvenu. Here and there, the profiles of apparently token heritage buildings are hemmed in by rank upon rank of thrusting new towers. The view from afar, though, is misleading. On the periphery of and even deep in the sunless canyons downtown, you can find hidden treasure on the streets.

Vancouverites know this better than anyone. Their city holds a world of memories, a world in which the buildings play a prominent part. In response to my drawings in the *Sun*, I have heard from a couple who first met in the bell tower of the Holy Rosary Cathedral, a lady whose "dad and his father built the Madrona Apartments on West 15th Avenue," and the designer of the neon sign at the Niagara Hotel—who, after seeing my drawing in the paper forty years later, took new pride in his work. A "native daughter of Vancouver" wrote to share her memory of "visiting the art studio of our Girl Guide captain in the turret of the old Imperial Bank of Commerce building at Granville and Dunsmuir." "Great days" in the Sun Tower were recalled by a former journalist. He worked there decades ago with a "happy crew who did mad things and produced good papers," and who on Friday afternoon "moved over to the bar in the Lotus Hotel to drink till one a.m." For these people and many others, there is much more to Vancouver than its flashy skyline.

During the late 1880s, Vancouver developed as a late Victorian and Edwardian city, influenced largely by the arrival of the Canadian Pacific Railway. It was a colonial town that was well placed on the imperial "all red route," from Great Britain to the Orient, travelled by Canadian Pacific's trains and steamships. Some buildings in Gastown were erected at that time. Most of the city's surviving architectural heritage, though, dates from an extraordinary boom that began with the Klondike Gold Rush in 1897 and ended just before the First World War. By 1912, Granville Street—which in 1890 was "just a slit in the forest, a solid wall of trees on both sides"—had become truly metropolitan.

A local business directory published in 1908 blustered, "Vancouver, the Liverpool of the Pacific, is one of the municipal wonders of the Twentieth Century . . . Canada's most progressive metropolis . . . the Gateway to the Orient . . . aided by the boundless resources of the country . . . and the enterprise of its citizens." The community of 1000 in 1886 had, in little more than twenty years, grown to a city of more than 100,000 people.

But in 1912, a recession took the wind out of the city's sails and trapped the municipality in the economic doldrums, where it remained until after the Second World War. There was a brief Art Deco building boom in the late 1920s, but in the early 1950s, Vancouver still looked essentially Edwardian. When the Hotel Vancouver was completed in 1939, it dominated the city with not a modern but a turn-of-the-century presence.

Virtually all the buildings from the boom era still stood: the Romanesque warehouses, the Beaux-arts office blocks, the neoclassical railway stations and the Greek and Roman banks. Even today, because of past concentration of modern development west of Granville Street, much of this heritage survives. East of Granville, along Hastings and Pender, the core of the old city still exists. There are many more old buildings here than I could include in this book—the diverse, ad hoc facades of Chinatown alone could have filled these pages.

Most of the drawings reproduced here are of buildings in the city centre and its vicinity, where there is currently the most serious threat to the city's architectural heritage. The scouting party that succeeded in destroying the Georgia Medical-Dental Building was only an advance guard of the battalion of developers standing before the city gates. But there is also a strong contingent of people who argue for preservation. The campaign to save the Georgia Medical-Dental Building, for example, was a *cause célèbre*. After protracted debate, members of City Council were convinced that the new building would be somehow "better."

It will certainly be more profitable—the word that too often lights the fuse of destruction.

In a wider sense, old buildings too can be profitable, not only in modest financial return. In their variety and craftsmanship of obsolete decor, old buildings offer reassuring guarantees that civilized values still exist in an increasingly tawdry world. Weather-worn stones and antique facades are a physical link with the past, sustaining our sense of personal and shared identity. I often feel a kinship with dated places' anonymous, vanished denizens, their lives and experiences invisible but always present in fading walls.

While few modern buildings are likely to resonate in this way in the years to come, there are exceptions. Vancouver has been better served by modern architecture than some cities I know. Several 1950s buildings in the city are already admired: the B.C. Hydro Building on Burrard Street (recently declared a heritage building), the Canadian Imperial Bank of Commerce at Granville and Dunsmuir with its interior mosaic mural by B.C. Binning, the Customs Building across Pender Street from the Marine Building and the uncompromising, late-1960s MacMillan-Bloedel Building on West Georgia, are among the highlights of contemporary corporate and institutional architecture in Vancouver. Significantly, those buildings were designed in a purposeful, optimistic modernism. They have a strength and conviction largely absent in today's postmodern world.

Otto Wagner, the fin-de-siècle Viennese architect, once wrote, "The main reason that the importance of the architect has not been fully appreciated lies...in the language he has directed to the public, which in most cases is completely unintelligible." These words are still appropriate today, when it seems few architects can understand their profession's history, never mind explain to the public the art they practise. Yet architectural history is rich in sources that we can look to as we attempt to solve the complexities of modern urban life and planning. Heritage buildings, where they survive, are constant reminders of standards once held in high esteem. Too many new buildings, as Robert Louis Stevenson put it, "belong to no style, only to a form of business much to be regretted."

Robin Ward
Vancouver B.C.
August, 1990

Old Post Office Building
Vancouver

Four of Vancouver's historic buildings stand on this block, bounded by Granville, Hastings, Howe and Cordova Streets. Two, on Granville Street, are shown in this drawing: the Post Office of 1910 and its 1939 extension.

Back in 1910, this area, near the Canadian Pacific Railway Station and the CPR steamship terminal, was becoming the new centre of the city. Arriving by sea or on a transcontinental train, you could look south up a Granville Street lined with Edwardian banks and business buildings. And you would hear the symphony of the city—the hooting steamships, panting trains, clanging streetcars and the clatter of construction.

At times, there is still an old world metropolitan buzz around this area although its appearance has partly changed. In the 1950s, modern office towers took root, but enough old buildings survive at Hastings and Granville to preserve the distinctive look of the district. These buildings include the whole block now known as the Sinclair Centre, a Federal Public Works project of the 1980s. Here, four heritage buildings have been reused with a civilized respect for the past. Behind their restored facades, modern government offices and a shopping arcade have been built in a perfect blend of old and new.

By the time the Post Office Extension was built, Art Deco was quite passé. Derived from the *Exposition des Arts Décoratifs* held in Paris in 1925, the style was characterized by a blend of classical Greek and Egyptian motifs, jazz age imagery, Art Nouveau and the angular and streamlined geometry of the machine age. Add to this Mayan art, nautical motifs from ocean liners and Hollywood cinema style, and you had a recipe for architectural decadence unequalled except, perhaps, by the exuberant baroque of eighteenth-century southern Europe.

No wonder the Post Office shied away from the style. As late as 1939, Art Deco in its more extravagant forms was too outré for an institution like the Royal Mail. McCarter and Nairne's design is notably restrained, their Art Deco ornament discreetly applied.

The mandarins at the Post Office clearly couldn't quite make up their minds about the style of the extension at the foot of Granville Street. It looks as if every postie in the city delivered detailed suggestions. Local architects McCarter and Nairne drew up a compromise with this basically modern design, embellishing the walls with enough traditional and contemporary ornament to keep everyone happy.

Completed in 1939, the building has a steel frame dressed with neoclassical stonework—fluted pilasters, of the sort you find in Rome, capped with fountains of Art Deco detail. On the lower floors, a procession of Beaux-arts arched windows parades down Granville Street, picking up where the design of the 1910 Post Office next door left off.

McCarter and Nairne might have preferred to emulate the bustling Edwardian baroque of the original with a full-blown Art Deco version in the manner of their Marine Building (page 102). But the public servants at the Post Office were more conservative. The building they ended up with is suitably dignified, a purposeful and fastidiously detailed design, strong enough to have weathered some alteration and loss of symmetry during reconstruction.

Originally, the extension was joined to the older Post Office building. When the Sinclair Centre was built, a section of the facade was removed to create a new entrance between the two. The stonework was repositioned on the return and an ornamental window reinserted at the Granville/Cordova corner.

Post Office Extension
Vancouver, Robin Ward 1990

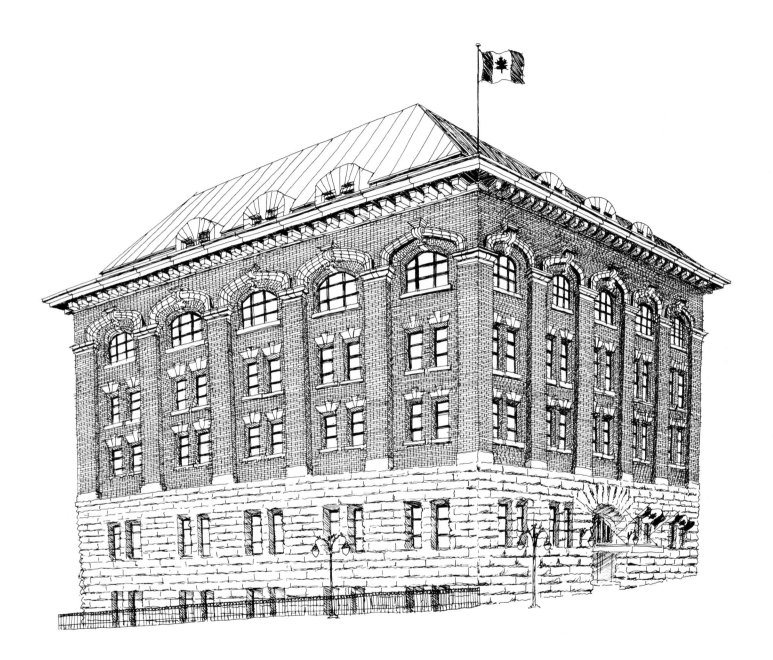

Customs Building, Vancouver
Robin Ward 1990

This formidable, Dickensian-looking structure was built at the corner of Howe and Cordova Streets in 1912 for Customs and Excise. Its presence is still as stern as the examining officers worked there.

The Customs Examining Warehouse, one of the quartet of distinguished old buildings which has become the award-winning Sinclair Centre, was completely remodelled within the existing facade. The other three buildings on the block—the Winch Building (page 18), the Post Office (page 20) and the Post Office Extension (page 14)—were similarly treated. The resulting architectural medley (each restored facade preserves a different style) is an inspired example of historical preservation, demonstrating the potential for reusing, rather than destroying, historic buildings.

There's more to the Sinclair Centre than just the old facades, though. Modern interiors within old buildings are often disappointingly bland or cloyingly imitative of past styles. But not here. The robust modern construction of the galleria inside plays an architectural counterpoint to the more delicate, individual notes of the period details. There's also a wonderful sense of both space and intimacy, as if in some medieval town in Europe, in the corridors, skylit galleries and nooks and crannies of this layered public arena.

Much of the costly interior rebuilding work involved in creating the Sinclair Centre passes unnoticed, the facades have been so well preserved. The structural steelwork meets seismic standards on buildings never designed with them in mind, and reconstruction from the inside out, while carefully propping up seventy-five-year-old facades, took years of effort to execute.

Many hidden treasures were discovered and retained during the process, giving the centre a sense of the past without compromising the modern design. There is no kitsch reproduction here. The dado-tiled corridors, classical columns, ornamental plasterwork, cast iron, Italian marble, Art Deco elevator doors and period decorative panels are all original.

Not every owner of an old building can afford this form of meticulous restoration without the benefit of the public purse, tax breaks or other incentives. The Sinclair Centre demonstrates the success that can be achieved.

No expense was spared on this 1909 office building on West Hastings Street, part of the Sinclair Centre.

Owner R. V. Winch, one of the city's early business moguls (he pioneered the salmon canning trade, built a mansion in the West End and drove about in a 1910 Rolls Royce), spent much of his fortune on this, his pride and joy, the first commercial building erected west of Granville Street. When built, it was the most up-to-date office block in B.C. But it didn't look it. Architects Hooper and Watkins went to town on the $700,000 budget and designed a Renaissance palazzo fit for a Florentine merchant prince.

They might have looked to contemporary rather than sixteenth-century Europe for inspiration. Winch and his kind, though, were not interested in the avant-garde, which was then storming the architectural salons there. They saw themselves as the Medicis of their day and chose to display their wealth and, in this case, good taste in traditional architecture. This is a building of restrained opulence and satisfying proportions. The eaves gallery with its free-standing colonnade, the arcaded ground floor and the interior marble and tilework are particularly fine features.

Hooper and Watkins, unlike their client, weren't entirely prisoners of the past. Behind the granite facade there is a modern steel and concrete frame. All the Renaissance stonework was for show.

The Winch Building, Vancouver
Robin Ward 1990

The Post Office Building
West Hastings and Granville
Vancouver
Robin Ward 88

Vancouver's former General Post Office Building on West Hastings Street looks as if it might be in Victorian Manchester or Glasgow, or on some Parisian boulevard. Its ornate Beaux-arts classicism (the Parisian École des Beaux-arts was the premier architectural school in nineteenth-century Europe) gives it an air of ostentatious, Victorian respectability. But it was built much later, between 1905 and 1910. In this respect, it is the archetypal colonial government building—built in a style twenty years behind the times.

It may have been dated when built, but it is an elegant, well-proportioned design which turns a difficult, sloping corner with panache and confidence. And it was built to a traditional urban scale, its height determined by stairs rather than elevators.

Inside, there was a spacious Edwardian post office with 1930s steamship-style fittings and a bibliothèque of brass mailboxes which was retained during the Sinclair Centre's construction. It was a wonderful place to post a letter. Unfortunately, it didn't survive more recent alterations.

The Post Office did survive a riot in 1938. The "floating population" of unemployed occupied this building and the local art gallery for four weeks before they were evicted by police. During the Depression years, Vancouver was the end of the line for many destitute unemployed workers. Some were branded "Red Revolutionaries" by fearful politicians and plutocrats, but while occupying the bourgeois halls of the art gallery, they never damaged the paintings.

Several local stone companies—some, like the B.C. Monumental Works, had names as imposing as the buildings—employed dozens of craftsmen to hand carve the sculptural and ornamental detail fashionable in Edwardian times. Many were immigrants: J. McIntosh & Sons, for example, from the original "Granite City," Aberdeen, and Portuguese and Italian artisans who brought their old world skills to the Pacific coast. The architectural details on the Post Office building's granite facade give Vancouver its most elaborate example of this virtually extinct art of masonry.

Today, looking at the rusticated ground floor, the colonnades with their carved Ionic capitals, the bas-relief heraldry within the curved pediments and the graceful clock tower topped by a symbolic sailing ship on the weathervane, you can see why the Vancouver *World* described this building as "palatial...a monument of chiseled stone and massive round pillars," testimony to "Vancouver's power and prosperity."

The most likable feature of the Court House is the two lions that flank what was once the main entrance on Georgia Street. To enter the building today, you go in the back door: that pleasurable sense of importance, of both the building's status (as the Vancouver Art Gallery) and one's approach to it, has unfortunately been lost in the change of use. The lonely lions guard a purposeless portico, a poor reward for their patience.

They were carved in 1910 by a Scottish artisan, John Bruce, employed by McDonald (stone cutters) of Main Street. Bruce modelled them after those by Sir Edwin Landseer, erected in 1867 in Trafalgar Square. Landseer's London lions were popular beasts, not only in Vancouver. Copies can still be found outside public buildings throughout the former British Empire.

Western civilization's concept and practice of law and order, as we know it today, has its origin with the Greeks and Romans. The style of their buildings was considered an appropriate manner in which to represent the dignified panoply of the law, banks and government institutions. Classical architecture too has its law and order, an unwritten constitution of harmony and proportion. Its laws are easily broken, its order difficult to attain.

Architect Francis Rattenbury, who in 1906 won the competition for the Court House with this neo-classical design, didn't break any laws here. But he didn't quite achieve the order which lifts a classical composition above the ordinary. He played all the right notes—a facade colonnade, columned and pedimented portico flanked by imperial lions, and a Palladian rotunda—to serenade the local judiciary with a flattering tune. But he lacked the skill and rigour, that hard edge of discipline and restraint, that sounds the chord of perfect classical proportion. The interior of the rotunda is more deftly handled than the building's outside detail.

Rattenbury's late-Victorian English sensibility was more at home with the romantic concoctions at which he excelled—the provincial Parliament Buildings and the Empress Hotel in Victoria, for example. But his Court House makes a fine art gallery, which it is today—a romantic and mildly subversive irony, given that art should challenge, as much as establish, order.

Old Courthouse, Vancouver, Robin Ward 1990

Canadian Pacific Railway Station, Vancouver
Robin Ward 1990

"In the nineteenth century, the railway station became a new gateway to the city, an imposing shape which stamped its mark on the landscape . . . the bud of new city growth."

This description rings true, particularly in western Canada where cities can trace their growth to the arrival of now absent trains. Most Canadian cities still have stations, echoing relics of a time of nation-building and visionary leadership. The railway companies and the government once knew where they were going. They built empires from sea to sea—none grander than that of the CPR.

Canadian Pacific originally built stations and hotels in Franco-Scottish baronial style, reflecting Canada's early cultural heritage. Their first major Vancouver station was built in this manner but was replaced in 1914 by the neoclassical structure still standing today on West Cordova Street.

This is one of the finest buildings in the city, a potent national symbol expressing the pride of its builders and the confidence and decorative taste of the time. Beyond the superb exterior colonnade is a magnificent neoclassical hall. Here, in place of carved Roman conquests, there are scenes of the Rocky Mountains, painted in romantic Victorian fashion and celebrating the landscape traversed by the trains.

There are no real trains here any more. But, saved from demolition, the building now houses offices, shops, cafes and the Seabus/Skytrain terminal—an adaptive reuse which ranks with the Sinclair Centre in standards of restoration.

Canadian Pacific Engine No 374, turntable
Vancouver BC   Robin W

The CPR Roundhouse, with its muscular interior of mighty cedar columns, is one reminder of the industry which covered the shores of False Creek. Formerly the industrial heart of the city, the area was once alive with lumber mills, rope works, railway sidings and engineering shops.

Much of the architecture of that era can still be seen on nearby Granville Island, magically transformed by a 1970s federal project that changed the man-made island (created in 1917) from a collapsing industrial zone to the recreational venue it is today. Early on in this process the decision was made to keep the old manufacturing sheds rather than sweep them away (as the CPR has done across the creek, where only the roundhouse still stands). This visionary manifesto allowed Granville Island's history and haphazard street layout to set the

This is the most famous steam locomotive in Canada, "the 'puffing billy' which made Canadian transcontinental railway history." Engine No. 374 pulled the first passenger train into Vancouver on the CPR's newly completed transcontinental railway in 1887, unquestionably the most important event in the history of the city. Miraculously, the locomotive, built at the CPR shops in Montreal in 1886, has survived to this day, largely through the

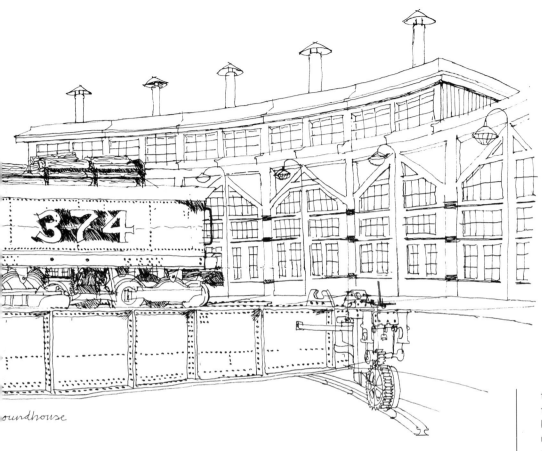

oundhouse

efforts of devoted individuals and organizations who supported her preservation at the CPR Roundhouse at the foot of Davie Street. Here, in appropriate surroundings (CPR's locomotives were once maintained in the 1888 building), No. 374 steams on, so to speak, as a "monument to the indomitable courage of the men who pushed the Canadian Pacific across Canada's plains . . . and the hitherto impassable mountains."

tone for the new development, which, in design terms, is appropriately "low tech." The public market, artists' studios, craft shops, glass blowers, printmakers, cafes and bars have installed themselves seamlessly in the architectural bric-a-brac of the district's industrial past. Even the railway lines have been retained.

There's no "great" architecture on Granville Island, but the vernacular collections of corrugated sheds, timber-beamed machine shops, cranes and a surviving cement works preserve the ambience of former days. This area has an evocative quality beneath the colour and activity of post-industrial times. When everything is closed, there's an aura of Pompeii about the petrified streets and silent sheds—as at the CPR Roundhouse, at once no trace and every trace of a bygone world.

Robin Ward 88

The railways had some cause to celebrate their arrival with gigantic stations. Yet they were pioneers in every respect but architecture. Even in the 1920s, well into the age of modern design, the language of architecture as spoken by Canadian Pacific and Canadian National was resolutely neoclassical. Canadian railway architects, like those

From the 1880s to the 1920s, the transcontinental railways played a fundamental part in the confederation and development of Canada. Aware of their role, and not modest about it, the railway companies built monumental stations to announce their arrival in major cities across the country. Vancouver's Canadian National Railways Station, crowned by typography as epic as the transcontinental journey, is a wonderful survivor of that era.

Completed in 1919 on land reclaimed from False Creek, and located some distance from the city centre, the CN station retains a frontier quality. There is no other building nearby: the station stands in majestic isolation. It's as if the railway, laid across the prairies, through the Rocky Mountains and down the Fraser Canyon, has just arrived. The restored, empty station seems brand new.

in nineteenth-century Europe and America, borrowed architectural styles from previous eras, lending their buildings an air of permanence and respectability. Above all, these buildings were symbolic. At a time when the frontier was still a reality, the sudden appearance of a railway station looking like ancient Rome was a clear manifestation of the civilization that the railways imported.

"I must go down to the seas again, to the lonely sea and the sky, and all I ask is a tall ship and a star to steer her by."

Occasional windjammers still berth at Ballantyne Pier, evoking the romance of billowing sails and creaking timbers, Cape Horn and the Roaring Forties, and China clippers from Asian shores.

Sailing ships were once a commonplace sight in Vancouver's harbour. The Spanish first explored this misty coast, followed by Captain Cook and his lieutenant, George Vancouver, who charted the Burrard Inlet in 1792. In the nineteenth century, sailing ships of the Royal Navy patrolled the fjords, maintaining a desultory claim to the territory on behalf of the British Crown. In port, their officers and crews would ignite the social calendar of the isolated colony.

Tall ships from around the world once loaded lumber at Hastings Mill and Port Moody. In their heyday in the late nineteenth century, square riggers bound for Australia and Japan, East Africa and Europe jostled at the quays, their masts and rigging a mirage of the logged forests replanted on the sea. Fabled China clippers once docked here, their cargoes of tea, silks and Royal Mail to be trans-shipped by the CPR to Liverpool, London, New York and Montreal.

This was the era of Gastown's prime. Dozens of saloons catered to a rough-and-ready clientele eager to drown the memories of back-breaking labour on the high seas. The ships, though, were icons of preindustrial craftsmanship and ingenuity. Moored at Ballantyne pier, this modern sail training ship conjured up visions of a vanished world.

Ballantyne Pier, built in 1921–23 across the railway tracks from Powell Street, is Vancouver's most impressive group of waterfront warehouses—four functional storage sheds each embellished with a colossal facade designed in the muscular industrial classicism of the nineteenth century.

Port buildings, like Victorian railway stations, were often built as impressive gateways. Ballantyne Pier is no exception. Even in dilapidation, these splendid buildings bespeak monumental notions of imperial trade routes, first class cabins topside and sweaty stokers below.

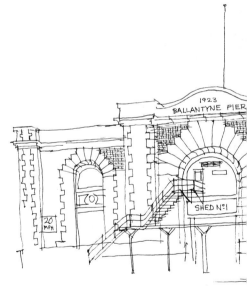

Ballantyne Pier, Robin W

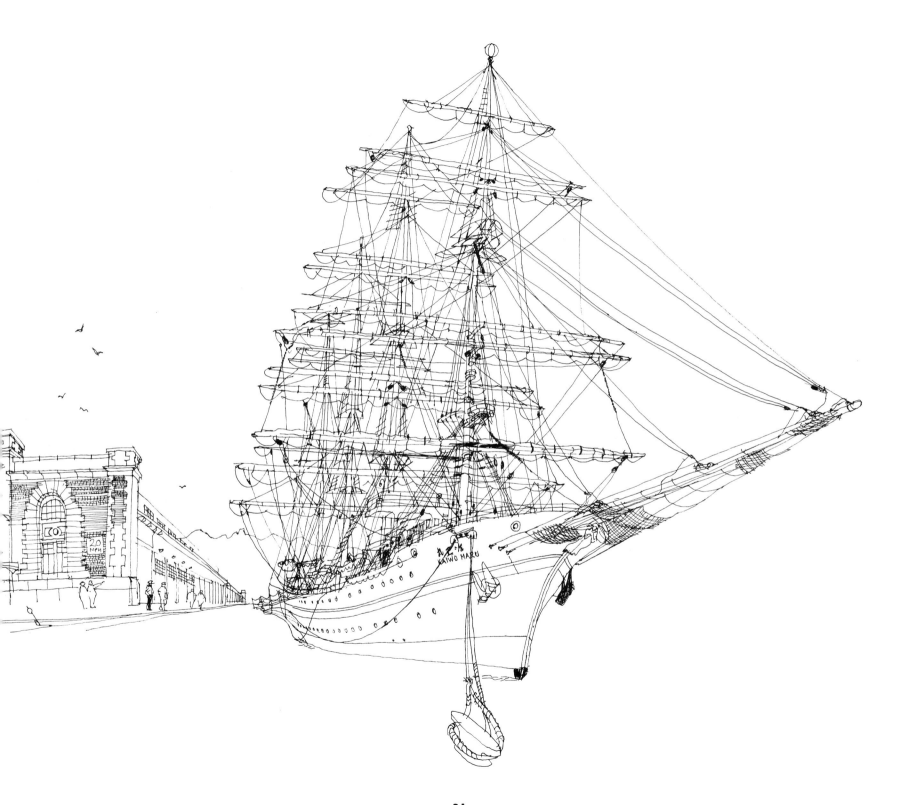

Hastings Mill, Vancouver
Robin Ward 1990

This picturesque wooden building in Pioneer Park, at the north end of Alma Street, is the oldest pioneering building in Vancouver. It dates from 1865, a time when the largest man-made objects in the town were the tall ships loading at the sawmill. The mill, the city's first industry, was located just east of Main Street on the Burrard Inlet. When it closed in 1929, few people recognized its importance.

Fortunately, the Native Daughters of B.C. did. This group, an historical society of pioneering, not native Indian stock (in 1919 when their organization formed, the worthy daughters saw no irony in their chosen title), saved the mill store. They needed a clubhouse, and the building was put on a barge and floated to its present site in 1930.

The store once had a false front, wild-west style, and was built on stilts over the water. These features were altered when the old mill store was rebuilt and became the Musem of B.C. Historical Relics in 1932. Inside the building, there is a wonderful collection of historic bric-a-brac, randomly displayed. By benign and unpretentious tenure and an apparent desire to display every antique item acquired, the Native Daughters, who still run the place, have inadvertently re-created the well-stocked jumble of the original store.

When the mill escaped destruction by the great fire of 1886, which wiped out Gastown, the store became a meeting place for the stunned citizens. They rebuilt their town in a year, in time for the arrival of the railway, and the first post office was established at the store in 1872 (you can still see the cookhouse bell that signalled the arrival of the Royal Mail).

"There used to be a great fleet of vessels in Burrard Inlet sometimes...they came from all parts of the world, some loading spars, some lumber, some shingles..."

Captain George Vancouver was the first European to note the vast stands of timber that attracted loggers to the Burrard Inlet in the 1860s. But it was the fur trade that drew the first pioneers here. In the late eighteenth century, Russian, Spanish, British and American mariners all sought the rich bounty of the north Pacific coast. Sea otter pelts found a ready market in Macau, and the Russians, who had colonized the Alaska coast, had begun to exploit this lucrative trade.

The Spanish, already established in California, claimed the B.C. coast. So did the British, who took tenuous title in 1795. Captain Cook navigated the coast in 1778, followed by George Vancouver. Alexander Mackenzie and Simon Fraser, exploring for the Montreal-based North West Company, arrived overland in 1793 and 1808 respectively. Fraser called the area New Caledonia, because the mountains and wooded coastline reminded him of his parents' Scotland.

The Hudson's Bay Company, having merged with the rival North West Company, established Fort Langley in 1827 as a tidewater outlet for furs from the interior. This settlement and the founding in 1843 of Fort Victoria strengthened Britain's claim to the territory, which became the Colony of British Columbia in 1858.

Lansdale and Aberdeen Blocks
North Vancouver Robin Ward 1990

North Vancouver was once called "The Ambitious City" but history shows it's really the great might-have-been. The first sawmill on the Burrard Inlet was built here in 1862, near the first white settlement on the inlet. This town, named Moodyville, rivalled Gastown for a time: by 1882 it had the first electric lighting north of San Francisco. The original mill closed in 1901 but by 1911 there was a budding commercial district on lower Lonsdale Avenue, and shipyards and new lumber mills. In Edwardian North Vancouver, as Moodyville was renamed, the talk was of telephones and tramcars, mighty thoroughfares and grand boulevards.

But it was mostly hot air. Grand Boulevard never became the Champs Elysées and the mighty thoroughfares are today pleasantly residential. The city's confident boosters and flamboyant speculators were deflated by the recession of 1912 and the First World War.

Bank of Hamilton Chambers and the adjacent Aberdeen Block, both dating from 1910, hint at an Edwardian building boom which never made it farther up the hill. Both, on Lonsdale Avenue, are distinguished buildings (the former Bank of Hamilton even has its original elevator, the first on the North Shore). Along with a handful of other nearby period structures, they form an historic core to the stillborn city centre.

North Vancouver Ferry No. 5 was built by the West Coast Salvage and Contracting Company and launched at Coal Harbour in 1941. (Coal Harbour was once a thriving industrial area—the last shipyard, Menchion's, closed in 1990.) Ferry No. 5 never did quite sail the seven seas, but spent its career shuttling passengers and cars back and forth across the harbour, where the Seabus now runs, until 1958 when the harbour ferry service was abandoned. Since 1959, Ferry No. 5 has been preserved as a floating restaurant.

On board the ferry, which is moored at its old slipway at the foot of Lonsdale, there's still nautical ambience, tastefully understated. The feeling is that you're actually en route to Yokohama on one of the old Canadian Pacific Empress liners. The ferry boat's tongue-and-groove wood panelling and other fittings, including the engines, were retained during conversion. The most noticeable addition is the superb neon sign, at over thirty years old now something of a period piece itself.

Vancouver is a city of views: from downtown of sudden mountains and harbour vignettes; from the suburbs of an Atlantis of towers floating on the horizon.

This scene is one of my favourites. If you're lucky enough to live or work in some Gastown belvedere, you'll see a man-made range of mountains and canyons no less dramatic than the breathtaking peaks on the North Shore. By happy accident rather than design, the city has developed into a mirror image of its surroundings.

Historically, this is a particularly interesting scene. Time and progress have marched from the foreground to the skyline. The city, once no more than a huddle of tents and false fronts, was incorporated in 1886 near the bronze reincarnation of its most celebrated early inhabitant—"Gassy" Jack Deighton.

Gassy Jack's idea of civilizing the pioneer settlement was to build a saloon—a bawdy beginning for a town with a pinnacled, glistening skyline of hopeful sophistication. In 1886, there was one church and there were twenty bars. By 1889, though, an English visitor observed: "The extraordinary thing about Vancouver is that in the midst of all this wilderness it is so absolutely modern." This rings true even today. All the modern towers pale before the presence of the mountains and the threatening sense, beyond their snow-capped peaks, of a wild and desolate interior.

Gastown, Vancouver
Robin Ward 1988

The Landing (former Kelley, Douglas & Co)
West Cordova and Water Streets
Vancouver. Robin Ward 89

Quite a number of offices and warehouses in the Gastown area were built with gold rush money, after city merchants struck it rich by supplying prospectors with provisions and equipment during the Klondike pandemonium of 1898.

Wholesale grocers Kelly, Douglas and Company had prospered in this way and in 1905 they built a new five-storey warehouse on Water Street. Between 1911 and 1914, they extended the building to its current size in response to Vancouver's rising economic stature. The city was becoming an important distribution and trans-shipment point between Europe, Canada and the Orient.

It's an impressive structure, easily the largest of its type in Gastown. Severe, classical proportions are drawn round three angled corners. Inside, as with most Gastown warehouses, the building is framed not with steel, but with a forest of massive cedar columns. The brick and granite facade is unadorned with the Edwardian detail you might expect here, giving the Kelly Building a clean, almost modern appearance. Aesthetically, this quality has contributed to the success of "The Landing," the polished retail conversion that has given the Kelly Building a new name and a new lease on life.

Unusually, there are two facades here, one on Cordova Street (right) and another (below) on Water Street, Gastown's main thoroughfare. Also shown (right) is the triangular Horne Block of 1889. J. W. Horne was Vancouver's wealthiest citizen, a successful land speculator (who wasn't at this time in Vancouver's history?). He made the most of this leftover corner with this Victorian Italianate style building, once the most ornamental in the city.

Some delicate detail can still be seen on the ground floor, but the rooftop cast iron and corner cupola that lent the building its air of capricious charm have long since been removed. The hydro poles and the old rooftop water tower add a period touch to this scene.

Stonework that seems straight from the quarry gives the impression here that the builder's budget didn't permit a more polished facade. The stone blocks, though, were carefully and deliberately chiselled by local and immigrant masons to create the rough-hewn effect.

You can date buildings by observing their style and use of materials. This warehouse in Gastown, for example, can be identified as a building from the 1890s. Its Romanesque style originated in twelfth-century southern Europe and was reinterpreted and popularized by American architect H. H. Richardson in the nineteenth century. Romanesque Revival soon became the fashionable dress for facades across the continent. In Canada, Toronto's old City Hall and CPR's Windsor Station in Montreal were influential examples.

Characterized by generously arched doorways, rusticated stonework and medieval carved capitals, Romanesque's chunky solidity seemed particularly suited to nineteenth-century North America, especially out west. Like most imports, the style had European antecedents and could be worked into powerful compositions. It imposed itself on streetscapes much as the immigrants did on the land.

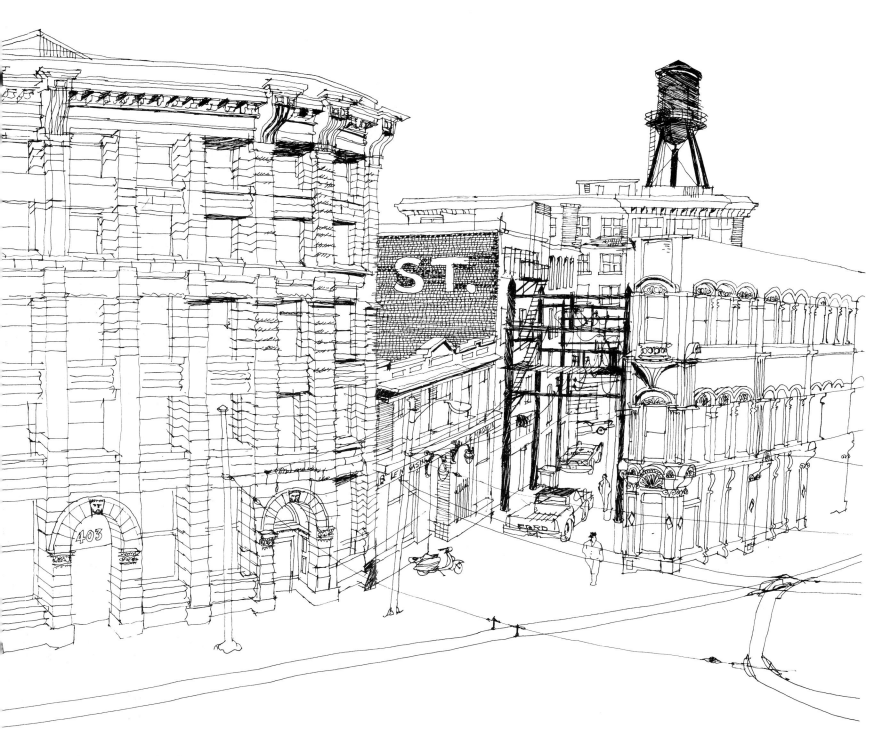

Cordova Street, Gastown
Vancouver, Robin Ward 1990

Hotel Europe, Powell and Alexander Streets, Vanc
Robin Ward 89

Few buildings in Vancouver have the dramatic presence of the Hotel Europe. Originally it was to have been two storeys higher but it still looks like a great ship that has ploughed ashore and beached itself at the narrow corner of Powell and Alexander Streets in Gastown.

It was built in 1909 on an awkward triangular site, but conveniently close to the passenger steamship berths from which custom was anticipated. Architects Parr and Fee designed this distinctive and once quite distinguished hotel for Angelo Colari, an Italian proprietor whose name can still be seen carved above the Powell Street entrance.

Signor Colari was one of the pioneer hotelkeepers in Vancouver. He started with a wooden structure on the same site in 1886, when Water Street extended only as far as Cambie Street. Hastings Street was then in the bush, and the Hotel Vancouver site was a favourite place for hunting!

The hotel has been refurbished and now contains flats for local people. The first reinforced concrete building in Vancouver, it is notable for its well-proportioned brick facade, a sweeping classical cornice, crystal-cut glass and polished granite on the ground floor and a glorious tiled lobby which looks more like a Roman bathhouse. But the Hotel Europe's most memorable feature is the way it turns the corner—the Italian way, with elegance and panache.

Vancouver's Empress Hotel is a poor relation of Victoria's famous institution. This dowager long ago lost whatever fame her name may have conferred, although a trace of Edwardian confidence remains.

Before the First World War, Hastings and Main was still within the city centre and more respectable than it is today. The Vancouver Empress elbowed its way onto a narrow site here in 1912, crowning its eight storeys with a parasol of cornice which still gives the building a powerful presence evoked by its name.

The 200 block of East Hastings Street is one of many in the downtown eastside where jostling period facades and antique signs enliven the streetscape. The wooden gold rush facade at the centre of this drawing wouldn't look out of place in Barkerville, while the Ovaltine Cafe has a 1940s film noir atmosphere.

There's a rich heritage in this unplanned montage, which strengthens the modest attributes of the individual buildings. Grouped together, their personalities are as varied as the people on the street—on this block, an empress with a retinue of eccentric retainers.

Hotel Empress, East Hastings Street Vancouver. Robin Ward 1990

Tellier Tower, East Hastings Street, Vancouver
Robin Ward '89

The ten-storey Tellier Tower (formerly the Holden Building of 1911) on East Hastings Street was once one of the most important buildings in the city. From 1929, it was Vancouver's City Hall, until 1936 when the administration moved to their million-dollar office block on West 12th Avenue (page 108).

I know why the bureaucrats left. This is a hazardous area, especially for drawing. I counted ten drunks, one of whom lurched into the shop doorway where I was standing. But I also had an appreciative audience of local people. The downtown eastside is a community—one with a stoic self-confidence formed by the comradeship of the canneries and the shipyards and on freight trains and logging booms.

Tellier Tower is a shining symbol of this community, having been completely refurbished in 1988 as a co-operative residence for local old folk. The Downtown Eastside Residents Association organized this government-funded scheme and carefully restored many of the building's architectural features.

Gerald Tellier, after whom the building was renamed, was a merchant seaman and trade unionist who worked in the relief camps of the 1930s. The new name is not without irony: the original owner, William Holden, a real estate and investment broker, was one of the wealthiest capitalists in the city.

There are still hard times in the downtown eastside. This is the Vancouver most tourists don't see unless they've been told about the Only Seafoods Fish and Oyster Cafe. Established in 1924 (the menu says 1912), the Only is worth savouring along with the district's tumbledown architecture.

Some buildings have been restored here, but not the former Woods Hotel, to the right of the Holden Building. Built in 1906 and then reported to be the best managed in western Canada, it lost its corner turret long ago. As the Pennsylvania and now the Rainbow, it declined with each change of name. The ripple of oriel windows which continues around the corner into Carrall Street, though, is still a striking feature.

This area is Vancouver's Skid Road, a term that once had a less pejorative meaning. Skid Road was a loggers' phrase referring to the cut pathway along which logs were "skidded" on wooden rollers—and, through time, any area where unemployed men gathered in the city between seasonal jobs.

BC. Electric Building, Vancouver
Robin Ward 89

The B.C. Electric Railway Company built this handsome office block at the corner of Carrall and Hastings Streets in 1912. At that time, B.C. Electric operated the most extensive interurban tramway system in Canada. Somervell and Putnam designed this steel-frame, brick and terra-cotta edifice in elaborate Beaux-arts style, originally with an expansive Parisian roof line and more sculptural detail than finally applied.

It was also designed as a tram depot. Travelling along Hastings Street, you might suddenly have found your tram lurching in to what is now the Bank of Montreal, where some routes terminated. You might also have found your progress delayed by a CPR freight train. CPR's privileges in this city once permitted steam locomotives to jaywalk across the streets. A spur line from Burrard Inlet to False Creek crossed Hastings at this point before the Dunsmuir Tunnel (used by Skytrain now) was bored in 1931.

The tramway system was abandoned in the 1950s but you can still see the track area round the back of the building. Inside, many original features have been preserved, including, behind three magnificent iron gates on Carrall Street, a superb Edwardian lobby.

Scottish-American steel baron Andrew Carnegie, the capitalist who gave his fortune away, funded this library. It was completed in 1903 at the corner of Hastings and Main Streets.

G. W. Grant, an architect who practised mainly in New Westminster, designed it in broad Romanesque style and capped it with a French Second Empire mansard roof. The corner, with its lantern, dome and columned entrance, boldly emphasizes this building's institutional self-importance. Like many Carnegie Institutes around the world, this one still stands as a symbol of dignified, high-minded Victorian philanthropy. Paradoxically, though, it is now the flagship of Skid Road.

Inside, in marble decrepitude, stained glass Shakespeare, Sir Walter Scott and Robert Burns greet an unexpected clientele. The city's poor and transient population are the main users of the community centre and library, giving the building a volatile, socialist ambience. It's as if a dissolute civilization has collapsed and its disenfranchised have infiltrated its relics, like Petrograd after the Russian Revolution.

Carnegie Library
Hastings & Main, Vancouver
Robin Ward 1990

Heritage Hall, Main Street
Vancouver, Robin Ward 88

Heritage Hall has a roof line and a facade straight out of provincial France or Montreal. There is a story that it was never supposed to be here at all, that back around 1914 an Ottawa official sent plans for Postal Station C to Vancouver instead of Regina. Mount Pleasant received a post office much larger and more ornate than necessary.

A more likely explanation for its unexpected grandeur and unlikely suburban location is that the Edwardian expansion of the city centre went west and not, as anticipated by Mount Pleasant's boosters, up Main Street. This downtown change of address left the Main Street post office like a wrongly delivered parcel, dilapidated and forlorn.

Happily, the building has now been beautifully restored as a community arts and social centre. Many of its French Renaissance features were retained. The facade is lavishly set with columns and pilasters, and mysterious, weatherbeaten carved faces stare from the stone. The Second Empire roof line is punctuated by an impressive corner clock tower capped by an Art Nouveau wrought-iron finial. The doorway is palatial enough to be on a town hall. Even the clock, manufactured in England by the makers of London's Big Ben, has been carefully overhauled.

Heritage Hall's clock is the last remaining mechanical public clock in the city. The similar Post Office clock at the Sinclair Centre is now electrically operated, its antiquated, redundant mechanism displayed in the shopping arcade below. At Heritage Hall, though, someone climbs up into the belfry every week to wind up the clock, which still chimes harmoniously every hour.

In the Victorian age, public clocks spread throughout Great Britain and its Empire, following the completion of Big Ben at the Houses of Parliament in London in 1859. Time was money in the nineteenth century world of industry and commerce, especially following the development of railways, factories, offices and government services. Railway timetables had to be precise, as did the postal service and working hours.

For Victorian architects, the clock tower was a novel and irresistible feature which lent a decorative, idiosyncratic quality above their facades. Canada's most famous clock tower is on the Parliament Buildings in Ottawa, completed in 1865 and rebuilt after a fire in 1916. In style and symbolism, Heritage Hall's tower owes much to the Ottawa design.

"**The first white men** to set foot in this wilderness were the Royal Engineers when they cut a road from New Westminster to the English Bay anchorage in the year 1860."

In 1867, Captain Edward Stamp, who built the original Hastings Mill (then called Stamp's Mill), piped water on a primitive aqueduct from Mount Pleasant to the Burrard Inlet for the boilers of his steam-powered sawmill. The area's forest was cleared and, for a short time, Mount Pleasant was farmed. By the turn of the century, Vancouver's first suburb had grown on the slopes overlooking the early industries of False Creek to the city and mountains beyond. But progress passed it by after the First World War. At Main and Broadway, the architecture is still handsomely Edwardian. Several old churches and pristine homes, some with columned verandahs and gingerbread gables, can be discovered here, particularly on West 10th Avenue between Main Street and City Hall.

Many older apartment buildings in Vancouver were designed in grand style—none more so than Quebec Manor (originally Mt. Stephen Apartments), built in 1912 at Quebec Street and East 7th Avenue.

These buildings were invariably planned with a degree of knowing pretension, allowing residents to imagine themselves in Edwardian Europe rather than in a young Canadian city still close to the frontier. The wrought-iron balconies, oversize, pedimented doorway and tiled entrance hall with its baroque, double height inner door recall the elaborate architecture of Belle Epoque apartment buildings in Paris and Vienna.

Quebec Manor also recalls a lost age of craftsmanship. The dazzling brickwork, hallway tiles, woodwork, cornice brackets and overall attention to detail are features rarely found today. Even more unusual are two unexpected permanent residents—the scantily dressed maidens (styled after Greek caryatids) who hold up the doorway pediment. A twin of this Mount Pleasant building once overlooked English Bay at the corner of Davie and Denman Streets.

Quebec Manor, East Seventh Avenue
Vancouver Robin Ward 89

East Render Street, Chinatown
Vancouver, Robin Ward 1990

There's a bustling serendipity here, as colourful as the sauce bottle labels in the grocers' shops. Every conceivable service, from herbalist to hairdresser, can be found somewhere in the area's impenetrable jostle. It's like being adrift in Canton.

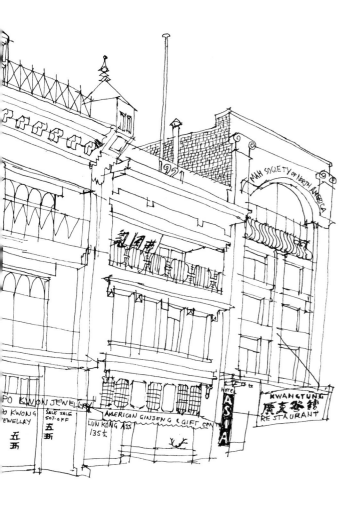

Chinatown's origin goes back to 1858 when gold was discovered on the Fraser River. Subsequent gold rushes enticed many Chinese from San Francisco and Hong Kong to British Columbia, where they worked mainly as camp followers in the towns and gold fields.

Victoria's Chinatown was larger than Vancouver's at this time, but by the 1880s Vancouver had become the main area of Oriental settlement. Over 10,000 Chinese were imported to help build the Canadian Pacific Railway through the Rocky Mountains. They are the unsung heroes of Canadian nation building.

Theirs was a society not wholly welcomed by the province that benefitted most from their labour. Chinatown's distinctive character was, paradoxically, strengthened in response to local prejudice. Chinese clan societies erected buildings that looked, above all, defiantly permanent.

These societies also provided social services— everything from letter writing to lodging. Wong's Benevolent Association built this elegant clan headquarters and Chinese language school on East Pender Street in 1921. Many of the buildings have large meeting rooms for social clubs and mah-jong players above the barber shops and cafes on the ground floor. This lively mélange gives Chinatown its special flavour, a dense urban mix and a traditional architectural fabric.

Chin Wing Chun Society Building East Pender St. Vancouver
Robin Ward 1990

Chinatown is a city of signs. At night, especially on East Pender Street, when they wink and flash in enigmatic conversation, it seems an insubstantial, floating world given form only by animated light.

Sometimes the signs are more interesting than the buildings they adorn. The Sun Ah Hotel suspends a giant, three-storey neon sign, complete with steaming noodle bowl, chopsticks and chubby typography, inviting peckish passers-by to Ho-Ho's Chop Suey. It's a vigorous design dating from the 1940s and enhanced by an equally lively name.

By contrast, the adjoining Chinese Benevolent Association displays more traditional Cantonese lettering befitting one of Chinatown's oldest buildings. Here the architecture is more notable than the signs. This 1909 building is one of the earliest to feature the recessed balconies, here framed by delicate iron railings, which give many Chinatown facades their distinctive character.

Recessed balconies are a traditional feature of architecture in southern coastal China, providing shade and a viewpoint to the street. In the 1925 Chin Wing Chum Building, European details added to the facade are reminiscent of the Sino/Portuguese style found throughout Southeast Asia.

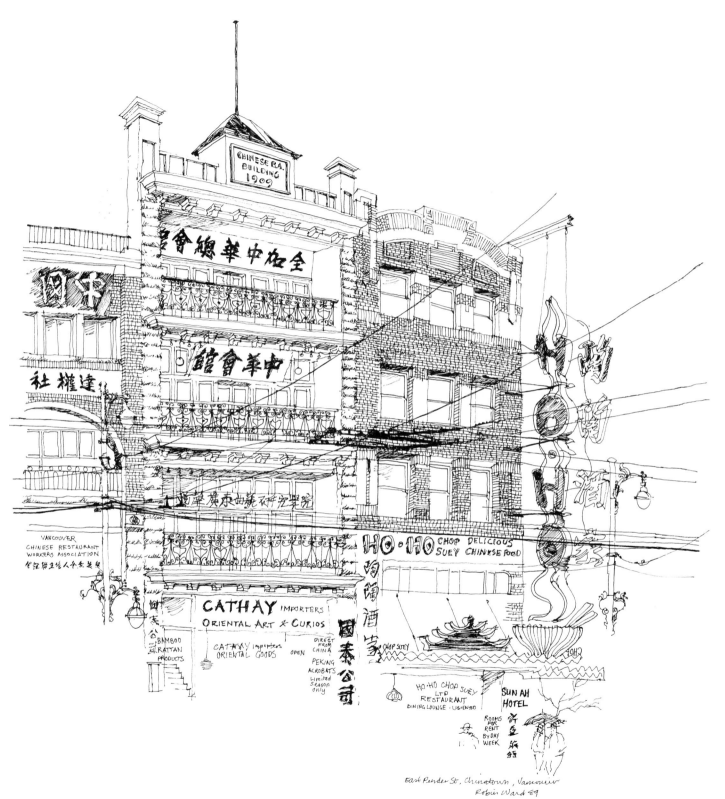

632 West Broadway, Vancouver
1150 Robson, Vancouver

Street was raided by police last night, ese all escaped by a trap door." There , illegitimate quality to Chinatown at he century. Pender Street (also known Street) and Shanghai Alley, with their , illegal lotteries and "loose women," its for most people. An opium factory uite openly across Pender Street from am Kee Building (far left) now stands. tivities confirmed many self-righteous ites in their prejudice against the ney called for "fearless enforcement places of vice," although most Chinese ectable and hard-working cooks, farmers and labourers.

the district had been cleaned up to the he Vancouver Tourist Association could d that visitors see "picturesque ." The same year, a mob of white protesting against "cheap Chinese ok that advice and trashed the area. n escaped a worse assault in the 1960s raffic planners proposed to bulldoze a hrough the area. Widespread public inst this, and a related threat to Gas- nately saved both of these historical d Vancouver from concrete strangula-

The Sam Kee Building is Chinatown's most unusual and famous facade. Facade is the word, because that's about all there is. This 1913 building is only six feet wide.

When the city widened West Pender Street, the Sam Kee Company's grocery warehouse was demolished, leaving a narrow plot for which the city refused to compensate the owner. Sam Kee was a feisty fellow, who had smuggled in rifles and ammunition after the 1907 riot. Stung by the city's summary treatment of his interests, he decided to rebuild anyway. He hired an (anonymous) architect to solve the one-block-long, six-feet-wide problem. Whoever the architect was, he deserves to be known: deliberately or inadvertently, he designed the "Thinnest Building in the World."

It's also the only building I know that looks and feels like one of the double-decker trams that shoogle along the streets in Hong Kong. Inside, the space is unbroken from end to end. Bay windows on the glazed facade of this ingenious design create a surprisingly spacious and luminous interior that has been well served by recent restoration.

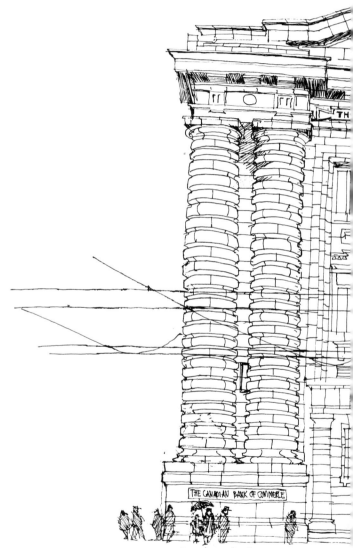

THE CANADIAN BANK OF COMMERCE

Canadian Bank of Commerce, Main
Vancouver. Robin Ward '88

Architects have often added Greek columns to their buildings to create a monumental effect, but here the building seems to have been added to the columns. They are on such a scale that Buckingham Palace or, at least, a railway station ought to sprawl behind the facade, rather than a medium-sized branch of the Canadian Imperial Bank of Commerce.

This hefty name, though, is matched by the scale of the four banded Doric columns, doubtless the bank's intention when this branch was built at the corner of Main and Pender Streets in 1915. Despite its completion date, the building's design is redolent of the nineteenth century: architecturally, Vancouver is really a nineteenth-century town whose monumental structures weren't built until the twentieth century. The Bank of Commerce, for example, may have been modelled on the Musée de l'-Orangerie building, constructed in Paris in 1853.

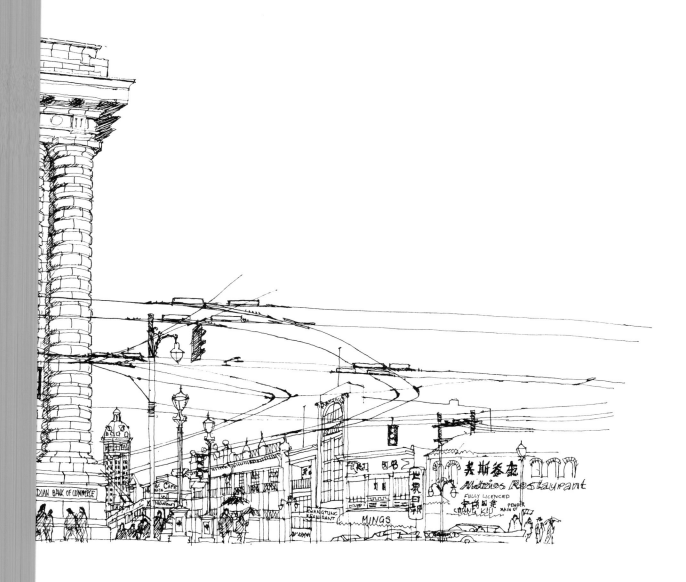

Sun Building, Beatty Street
Vancouver. Robin Ward 88

a solitary light on high up in the Sun
he Sunday evening when I finished this
A spectral newsman perhaps, shirt-
f in the tropics, clattering out Monday's
old typewriter. In the gloaming, the city
e on. Trolley buses hummed along the
ets. The run-down hotels, the old ware-
t lonely light—the area took on the am-
fty years ago.

ries were once written here. The *Van-*
was published in this building from
ing its name and memories when it
e Granville Bridge to the new Pacific
ling in 1964.

r Louis D. Taylor wrote himself into the
ry books with this colossal structure, a
as Vancouver's mayor and the subse-
cial trouble that forced his paper—the
World, for which this tower was built—
ut in 1917. "There is no limit to the
s of the city," he once declared, his sky-
wspaper tower evidence of Vancouver's
etropolitan status.

a *Citizen Kane* ring to this story, and to
this building. With a facade as bold as a
dline and a tower that punctuates the
nder corner like a giant exclamation
s building was designed to be seen
t its newspaper's circulation area—the
and the publisher's prominence symbol-
hitecture.

In 1912, when it was built for the Vancouver *World*, the Sun Tower was, briefly, the tallest in the British Empire. It may also have been the most risqué. The facade is embellished with naked caryatids, sensuously posed, who support the cornice above the arcaded gallery halfway up the building.

Victory Square is architecturally and topographically the most interesting surviving Edwardian public space in Canada. All around on the sloping square are the relics of dismantled empires—the Dominion Building, the Sun Tower and the corniced view down Hastings Street towards Woodward's department store. There's a tingling sensation of times past as you walk these listless streets—the area has remained unchanged since the First World War. Marble lobbies and Beaux-arts stonework testify to civic boosters and the wealth that once circulated here, while at the Cenotaph across Hastings Street there is the sadness of soldiers' extinguished dreams.

"Here stood HAMILTON first Land Commissioner, Canadian Pacific Railway, 1885. In the silent solitude of the primeval forest he drove a wooden stake in the earth and commenced to measure an empty land into the streets of VANCOUVER."

Lauchlan Alexander Hamilton was the Scottish surveyor employed by the CPR. He is remembered at Victory Square on a bronze plaque fastened to the building at the corner of Hastings and Hamilton Streets. Hamilton's grid flies off at an angle from the Gastown streets as it follows the shoreline. Odd angles and skew-whiff corners give the intersections here a lively spatial character. Victory Square isn't really square at all, due to Hamilton's inspired realignment.

Designed in ebullient 1890s Chicago commercial style, the 1910 Dominion Trust Company Building, begun by the Imperial Trust Company, was once the tallest in the British Empire. Its pre-eminence didn't last long in the booming city of the time—the Sun Tower (page 64) took the title in 1912. From a distance, the Dominion Building looks like the tallest bar of toffee in the British Empire. Its steel frame is thickly coated with red brick and terra-cotta tiles.

The architect, one J. S. Helyer, took a fatal fall down the ornamented stairwell (perhaps when he saw the result of his labours). He had certainly had a good chew over the decorative details: two massive Corinthian columns and Adamesque scrollwork, cheeky cherubs and a concave, curlicued cornice are topped by a mansard roof copied from a Parisian boulevard.

Surprisingly, the result is quite elegant, even impressive, particularly the way the building boldly dominates the West Hastings/Cambie Street contour—a topographical effect that enlivens streetscapes all over the city. Imperial Trust, intending to build the newest and finest office building in Canada, succeeded to an extent. The Dominion Building is the queen of the city's Edwardian business blocks. Inside, the lobby and interior are well preserved. A nice period touch is the recently installed smoke shop at the front entrance.

Dominion Building, West Hastings St.
Vancouver, Robin Ward 89

Birks Building
at Georgia & Granville

rguably the finest of all Vancouver's
buildings. It was designed by Somervell
m, a Seattle partnership, who were
most able architects working in Vancou-
time. It was an exquisitely composed
its ground floor canopy to the neo-
e window treatment and delicate cor-
e top storeys. Tiled with decorative
a and gracefully turning the Geor-
le corner, it was as fabled in Vancouver
treal-based jewellery store inside.
t you at the clock" was a commonplace
lay, only the cast iron clock, made by the
mpany of Boston, remains. Birks al-
lemolition of their building in 1974.
s clock is a fine example of decorative
iral cast iron—an unusual feature on the
streetscape. By Edwardian times, cast
en replaced by steel as a structural com-
l by terra-cotta for ornamental details.
nineteenth century, when cast iron was
ouver's builders tended to use timber
r internal supports. Some older shop-
istown, though, are partly cast iron, but
net can detect it beneath layers of paint.
once produced large quantities of cast
, particularly in Glasgow and New York,
mail-order catalogues from which you
choose complete buildings, as elaborate
nce palazzi, made from this material.

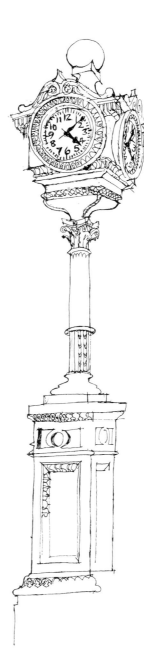

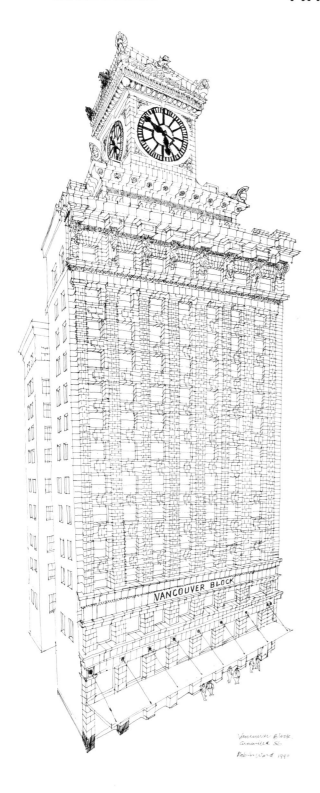

Architect W. M. Somervell, who designed the Birks Building (page 68), once declared of architects: "No matter how businesslike and practical we choose to be, we are essentially artists." Architects Parr and Fee's work, by contrast, was advertised as "the production of buildings that will pay...*Utilitas* is their motto and revenue their aim."

It is ironic that Parr and Fee's most visible work still stands next door to where Birks used to be. In a triumph of Edwardian exuberance over architectural quality, it is their Vancouver Block that survives today.

I like this building, though. It has a vulgar style that symbolizes the rampant growth of Vancouver in the early 1900s—it looks like a tiered wedding cake with its icing of terra-cotta. Caryatids support the cornice and Greco-Roman ornament frames the clock. There is no good reason for this decor other than flamboyant one-upmanship and questionable taste.

At fourteen storeys, this 1912 building couldn't rival the Sun Tower (page 64) as the tallest in the Empire, but it may have had the biggest clock. There's no excuse for missing an appointment here.

Hudson's Bay Company

Hudson's Bay Department Store, Vancouver
Robin Ward 88

ugh terra-cotta here to tile a thousand
. This gigantic emporium was built be-
and 1926 in the colonnaded, neoclassi-
t became a Hudson's Bay trademark (an
tical store was built in Victoria during
eriod, and Calgary and Winnipeg boast
mples).

ent Hudson's Bay store (the third in the
ilt in two parts. Until 1925, the original
ng, at the corner of Georgia and Gran-
, adjoined the eastern half of the new
oked a bit like a four-storey relation of
nnes-Thompson Block (below), which
three blocks north on West Hastings
couver's streets were once lined with
uildings of this type, their unsophisti-
n a combination of frontier vigour and
an pretension.

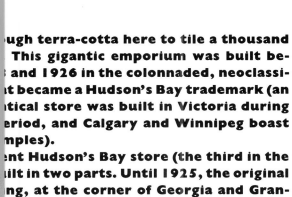

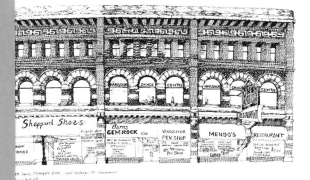

Department stores, where you could buy almost everything under one roof, were a nineteenth-century French innovation. The first, the Bon Marché, was built in Paris in 1876 and the idea spread throughout Europe and North America in late Victorian times.

The Hudson's Bay design owes something to London's Selfridge's, a near contemporary, which set the standard for lavish Edwardian stores of this type. The Bay's construction brought a degree of metropolitan European sophistication to the west coast, but the company remains true to its fur-trading origins. The store may be fragrant with Parisian perfume on the ground floor, but upstairs you can still buy point blankets, the traditional HBC trade item bartered for pelts in the North.

Jonathan Rogers was a founding father of the Vancouver business community, having arrived in town in 1887, on the first CPR train. He was an influential member of the Parks Board for twenty-five years and served as president of the Vancouver Board of Trade. Unlike some of his more avaricious colleagues, Rogers was a public-spirited man, and something of a philanthropist, leaving much of his fortune to good causes.

Vancouver's resident architects couldn't cope with the amount of work available during the city's Edwardian building boom, and several Seattle architects gained commissions here at that time. One of them, Warren A. Gould, was hired by Welshman Jonathan Rogers, a prominent local resident, to design this handsome Beaux-arts commercial block at the corner of Pender and Granville Streets.

Seattle was also the source of the terra-cotta tiles, over 10,000 of them, that completely cover both street facades with a decorative veneer. But the building's most extraordinary feature was the basement barber shop. Vast, mirrored and tiled, it looked like a room in the Palace of Versailles.

The Rogers Building, Vancouver
Robin Ward 1990

SEYMOUR
BUILDING

525

CAREER
PERSONNEL
LTD

FRESH
ASSORTED
SANDWICHES
5TH

COMMERCIAL
LANDS
EXCEPT COMMERCIAL
VEHICLES

ONE
WAY

Seymour Building
Vancouver
Robin Ward '88

This soaring facade is one of Vancouver's earliest skyscraper designs. Most of the city's Edwardian office blocks are neoclassical, characterized particularly by heavy, decorative cornices which tend to bolt the buildings to the ground. Here, the ten storeys of Gothic terra-cotta tracery, dating from 1914, look as if they could climb forever.

This cathedral of commerce shows the influence, if not the scale, of New York's 1913 Woolworth Building. Skyscraper Gothic then became briefly fashionable. The Seymour Building, designed by Seattle architects Somervell and Putnam, is Vancouver's only true example of this style.

Tall buildings (anything higher than one could reasonably be expected to climb by stairs or which could be built with load-bearing timber, brick or stone) were made possible by developments in the late nineteenth century—structural steel framing and the invention of the elevator. Rapid growth in cities and the desire of businesses to be grouped together in the city centre led to the creation of downtown cores, in which competitive facades began to reach for the sky.

Chicago architects were the pioneers of this new building technique. In the 1890s, they wrestled with the compositional and stylistic problems tall buildings created. They copied Italian Renaissance campanili and later the setback style of Mayan ziggurats. But most applied the proportions of Greek columns, designing skyscrapers with a base (ground floor), shaft (middle) and capital (top floors and cornice). The Seymour Building plays a creative variation on this theme.

Before modern architecture discarded ornament in favour of structural honesty, architects were preoccupied with how to embellish their early skyscrapers. Their only reference was the past, so they made these new buildings look like Roman temples, Venetian palazzi, medieval town halls or Gothic cathedrals 20 storeys high. Some architects later succeeded in creating new styles more appropriate to tall buildings. But most, along with their clients, were gloriously adrift in history.

They found terra-cotta an ideal material to clad their steel-frame buildings. It was lighter than stone and easily moulded. Like nineteenth-century cast iron, it could be mass-produced to replicate virtually any pattern or architectural motif—cartouches, columns, pilasters, cherubs, cornices and Corinthian capitals.

While most of the terra-cotta in Vancouver was made in Seattle or San Francisco, that used in the 1913 Hotel Vancouver was an exception. The upper floors of this amazing building, a fifteen-storey Italian/Spanish hacienda demolished after the war, were elaborately clad in Doulton terra-cotta shipped from England. Messrs. Doulton of Lambeth, London, well known for their architectural terra-cotta, supplied larger-than-life buffalo and moose heads, corbels, balusters, friezes and other tiles for the hotel. I like to think that the buffalo and moose were saved and now lurk in some Shaughnessy garden.

This classic North American streetscape was the result of Vancouver's laissez-faire Edwardian building boom. Downtown development at that time didn't mean laying waste to whole blocks. Few local companies had the ability or need to do so anyway, and the big guns back east saw Vancouver only as an outpost of their empires.

New buildings were designed to fit existing lot sizes, which were originally determined by the CPR. The more ambitious designs shot up ten storeys or more, giving Edwardian Vancouver a clutch of tall, narrow facades, usually neoclassical in style, like the 1912 London Building shown here.

There's an architectural vitality and an authentic period aura in these irregular facades and cornices. Here they form an essential part of the surviving, historic downtown core.

West Pender Street, Vancouver
Robin Ward 1990

NOW AVAILABLE
BED & FULL BREAKFAST
COLORED
TV $24.35 ONLY

PRIVATE
BATHS
AVAILABLE

HOTEL
Restaurant
PUB
ON BOOKS

TOP EXOTIC DANCE SHOWS
ALL STARS · 10 BEST DANCERS
IN VAN. DON'T MISS THE
ACTION OPEN 11AM-1AM

Albion Books
used books
bought & sold

Jesus Saves

DAVIDSON
YUEN
PARTNERS

THE LUMBERMENS' BUILDING

509 RICHARDS

The area directly south of Gastown, from Victory Square to Granville Street's downtown office towers, seems to have slumbered for years. It's a jumble of parking lots and faded hotels, eminent Edwardian banks, office buildings and turn-of-the-century commercial facades. So far, the area has escaped the intrusion of corporate marble and fountained plazas or the sanitized historicism of the tourist trade.

A sense of traditional urban life and modest endeavour persists here among the small businesses, eccentric shops and secondhand bookstores. Many of the old buildings have that slightly dog-eared, historic resonance that is too often mistaken for a sign of lack of progress.

Down the lanes, which still bisect most downtown blocks, tantalizing, antique facades materialize. There is even a hint of the frontier, of a half-built city of random cornices arising from the tangle of timber poles and hydro wires.

There's a reassuring continuity both here and at Victory Square—a balance that sensitive restoration of buildings like the Lumbermen's Building (what a name!—their bank was on the ground floor) can help maintain.

The Lumbermans Building, Richards Street
Vancouver, Robin Ward 89

Some buildings in the older part of downtown remind me, in their way, of Roman ruins. Here are the columns and pedestals of collapsed empires and weary dynasties, the remnants of boardroom battles and eastern takeovers. The buildings themselves look like classical columns, especially where they stand in monumental isolation as the West Pender Building does. How confident it looks, even in decline.

Inside the 1912 building, there is a further resonance. From the columned entrance (the back of the building is shown here), through the marble lobby and up every floor, the interior seems to have remained unchanged for years.

Marble-tiled corridors, a brass Royal Mail box (Canadian Cutler Mail Chute Company of Montreal) fed by chutes from all floors, and varnished wood office doors each with frosted glass and painted company names, suggest a 1940s building whose tenants, à la Raymond Chandler, just had to be private eyes. The ground floor, formerly a two-storey banking hall with carved ceilings and pilastered marble walls (partly boarded and floored over now), still displays the most imposing bank vault I've seen—an Edwardian affair set in a neoclassical marble doorway.

The basement of the West Pender Building was once the location of the Vancouver Safety Deposit vaults, claimed to be the "Safest Armour Steel Vaults in the West." They were "Burglar and Fireproof" until January 1977, when a Montreal gang pulled off a daring, old-fashioned heist.

They broke into the building from the fire escape on the mezzanine on a Friday night. Over the weekend, they drilled and tunnelled through three feet of concrete and steel plate and ransacked 1200 safety deposit boxes inside. The gang made a clean getaway—as far as the airport, where their heavy baggage aroused suspicion. Airport staff discovered $2 million worth of bank notes, rare coins, jewellery and gold bullion. Police arrested the men, who had already boarded the Sunday evening flight to Toronto, but it was not until the following day, when the time clock allowed the vaults to open, that the cops knew what to charge the robbers with.

West Pender Building, Vancouver
Robin Ward 1990

Niagara Hotel, West Pender Street, Vancouver
Robin Ward 89

This scene is straight out of a 1940s black-and-white Hollywood film—when the streets were always wet, the cops were Irish and neon signs danced in the twilight.

The Niagara Hotel on West Pender Street perfectly evokes this ailing but exciting world of honest dames and private eyes. Its neon sign is a classic 1940s design, a Niagara of light cascading down the facade. The sign was made in Vancouver in the early 1950s by Neon Products of (Western) Canada and designed by employee Laurence Hanson, at a time when Vancouver had a reputation for its neon. At night, the cinema and dance hall signs made Granville Street glow like Broadway.

Neon is so inextricably associated with the North American urban landscape that it is a surprise to learn it was first displayed in Paris in 1910. Georges Claude perfected this form of illumination, and his company, Claude Neon, developed a franchise system that dominated world markets until the 1930s.

In the 1960s, the use of neon declined, partially eclipsed by the mass-produced, plastic world of corporate identities. Neon's idiosyncrasies (no two neon signs are alike) and the artistic skill necessary for its manufacture fell out of fashion. Recently there's been a revival, although few modern signs match the scale or virtuosity of the Niagara's work of art. Here, pine trees, rocks and tumbling waters glow and animate the night.

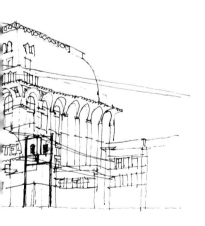

The **British Columbia** Permanent Loan Company, a name with a ring of aspiration and Edwardian confidence, was, like the Canada Permanent, quite modest in its architectural requirements. Architects Hooper and Watkins designed this scaled-down Beaux-arts bank, built nearby on West Pender Street in 1907. The building is toytown in its scale although mature in its neoclassical style and detail. I like to imagine that it was part of a much greater scheme to cover the whole block with imperious columns and porticos, like an American state capitol, of which only the entrance was built.

Were illusions of permanence abandoned here? The building lacks the scale and power its name implies. Inside, though, there's a real surprise. The original banking hall has survived. It is a larger and more impressive space than you expect to find, and its pièce de résistance is an almost Tiffany-style stained glass dome.

BC Permanent Loan Company Building, West Pender St.
Vancouver, Edward ?

Tucked away on Richards Street amidst the hydro poles at the back of the Niagara Hotel is one of the gems of Vancouver architecture.

Originally the Canada Permanent Building, it dates from 1912, and was designed by one J. S. D. Taylor. Its pedimented facade is typical of the solid classicism once favoured by banks and trust companies.

Here, the treatment is more inventive than usual. Taylor's classicism is symbolic and eclectic. The heavy pediment imitates a Greek temple. The facade's four Doric pilasters and the use of small columns to frame the upper floor windows show both Greek and Roman influence. The doorway, boldly off centre, features a baroque garland of fruit hung over a classical pediment. The frame, splayed at the base in ancient Egyptian fashion, rises through the pediment to enclose a clerestory window, picking up adjacent horizontals. This is a clever touch. So are the semicircular balconies, whose shape and Italianate ironwork lighten an otherwise weighty facade.

Inside, there's some fine wood panelling and carving that echo the exterior style. There is also lavish use of marble on the ground floor and staircase. There is even, as MacLeod's Books discovered when they moved in, the original bank vault with its dynamite-proof iron door.

The building's crowning glory, however (and its Canadian content), is the symbolic emblem of the Canada Permanent Mortgage Corporation—two beavers, and waves crashing on a castellated lighthouse tower.

Canada Permanent Building
Richards Street, Vancouver
Robin Ward 89

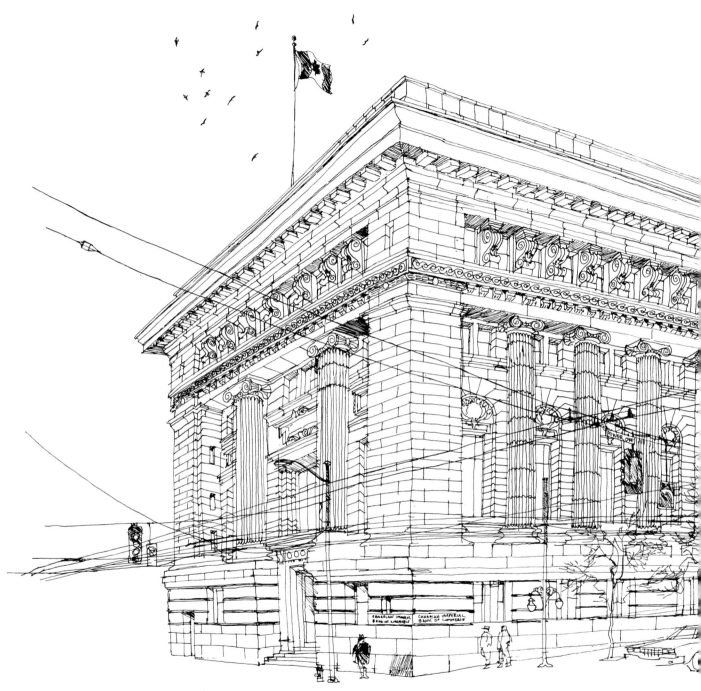

Canadian Imperial Bank of Commerce
West Hastings St. Vancouver
Robin Ward 89

I like a bank that looks like a bank—that is, like a Greek temple. I like the ritualized transaction conducted over mahogany counters in vast, marble, wood-panelled banking halls and the feeling of continuity and well-managed funds. Until the 1950s, the banks thought so, too. Classical architecture was respectable and it gave their buildings an aura of antiquity, stability and security.

Vancouver's financial district has a rich collection of these old-fashioned banks, grouped at the lower end of Granville Street. Among them is the Canadian Imperial Bank of Commerce, which retains its sense of dignity despite 1950s alterations to the interior. Fortunately, the facade remains much as it was when built in 1908. Designed by the Toronto firm Darling and Pearson, its massive, fluted Ionic columns, deep-set eaves gallery, heavy cornice and rigid adherence to classical style combine to create an impression of unimpeachable authority.

Architects Somervell and Putnam designed this elaborate bank at the corner of Granville and Pender Streets for the Merchants' Bank of Canada. It was built in 1916.

Somervell, an American, was one of the most prolific and talented architects working in Vancouver at the time. Two of his other buildings, both dating from 1912, the London and Seymour Buildings (pages 78 and 76), share this block with the Merchants' Bank, now the Bank of Montreal.

This civilized enclave of Edwardian architectural taste is an invaluable grouping of historical buildings. Not only do they give a flavour of the city during its Edwardian boom years, but also they show the range of Somervell's work (he was the creative force of the partnership). Somervell's European travels had equipped him to imitate classical and other styles. The architectural conservatism of his clients, mainly banks and trust companies, allowed his experience to mature with mannered displays of classical proportion and ornament.

The Bank of Montreal combines a forceful presence with a wealth of delicate detail—fretwork, corbelling, garlands, mouldings, anthemions and palmettes, lions and ornamental bronze window frames. It is arguably Somervell's finest work. Particularly precious here is the period interior, which remains largely unaltered.

In 1924, the bank enlarged the building with a new Corinthian columned entrance, three window bays up Granville Street and a coat-of-arms on the cornice, with head-dressed and feathered Indians. The alteration was accomplished so well that it's difficult to distinguish the addition from the original.

Bank of Montreal, West Pender and Granville Streets, Vancouver. Robin Ward 1990

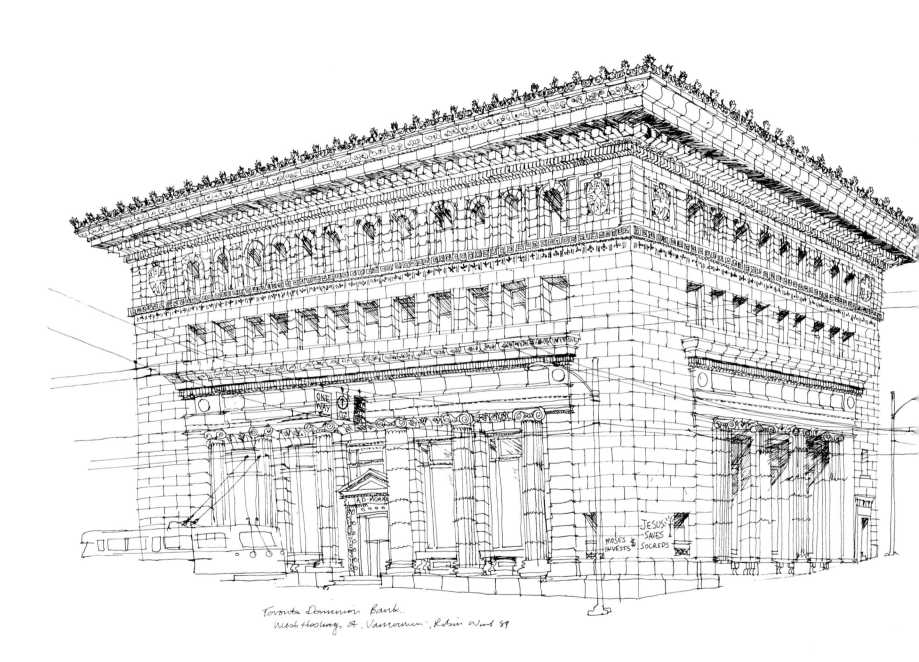

Toronto Dominion Bank.
West Hastings St, Vancouver, Robin Ward '89

Somervell and Putnam designed this neoclassical edifice at the corner of Hastings and Seymour Streets in 1920. 1920! If Somervell and Putnam or the Toronto Dominion Bank knew about modern architecture, which was then taking its first steps in Europe, it doesn't show. This building is resolutely traditional. They even proudly put the date on the door—in Roman numerals.

Banks tended to take a wait-and-see approach to architecture, following trends rather than setting them, exercising the same well-practised caution that normally characterizes their financial affairs. Somervell and Putnam had designed so many banks that they probably could have pulled this one out of a hat. But they seem to have been challenged here to design an original and opulent variation on the neoclassical theme.

This was the local head office of the Toronto Dominion Bank for many years. At the time of writing it stands in abandoned decay. Its facade may eventually be reused as part of a modern development, but I think it should be left as a monumental ruin, like the remnants of ancient Greece and Rome whose architectural styles it emulates.

The Chamber of Mines holds records of provincial mining history—photographs, maps, voluminous paperwork, mineral samples—deposited, like sediment from forgotten stopes, since the Chamber's foundation in 1912. They staked a claim to this building in 1959 (it was originally built for the Royal Financial Company in 1927) and painted gold lettering on the window, suggesting the dreamed-of mother lode. The building was an appropriate choice: there's a hint of a lost civilization on the arcane terra-cotta facade, a sort of remnant of the Eldorado that explorers long for.

Inside, there's a sense of studious excitement amidst the rock samples and glass cases. On the wall, a mountainous relief map of B.C. daunts would-be gold-seekers with the rumpled *terra incognita* of the province's interior. The map was once shipped to London to persuade British investors to risk their money in the potentially rich province. Architecturally, though, Eldorado is right here. The Chamber of Mines recently polished and restored this little gem.

Buildings often represent the status and aspirations of their owners. Architects knew this, particularly in Victorian and Edwardian times, and they raided history books to bestow on their clients' buildings the wisdom of ancient Greece or the imperial might of Rome.

Credit Foncier Franco-Canadien of Montreal clearly saw themselves a cut above the average bank or trust company in 1914. They built this neoclassical palazzo to say so, writing their name in finely cut Roman typography on the entrance entablature.

This sort of commercial one-upmanship often produced bombastic buildings where size outweighed subtlety, but not here. The combination of ten storeys of finely cut stonework, twenty-six Corinthian columns (twenty-two fluted on the dramatic, recessed eaves gallery and four at the entrance), the pilaster-framed ground floor arcade and a highly decorative, copper cornice could have been a recipe for confusion. But as built at the West Hastings/Hornby Street corner by architects H. L. Stevens and Company, this is an architectural composition of eminence and distinction—the finest of its era in the city.

Just along from the Credit Foncier building, there's a frisson of the frontier deep in the corporate canyons of Vancouver's financial district. Every time I pass the British Columbia & Yukon Chamber of Mines on Hastings Street, I visualize grizzled prospectors and intrepid geologists staking claims in the wilderness. In fact, mining companies, adventurers and hopeful investors often begin their explorations here.

Credit Foncier Building
Vancouver
Robin Ward 88

Vancouver Club, West Hastings Street
Robin Ward '89

When Vancouver's business barons planned a new club building, constructed in 1913 with a view of the harbour, they looked to London for inspiration and to immigrant English architects Sharp and Thompson for a grandiose design.

The result was and still is the city's most opulent Edwardian building, a neo-Georgian design on West Hastings Street, emulating the aristocratic, nineteenth-century gentlemen's clubs of St. James. Architecturally backward-looking, the building represents an idealized, civilized past rather than the future, which, in other respects, its members bullishly embraced.

It's a convincing copy, conveying establishment privilege and the pompous complacency of Britain's imperial heyday. There's still an atmosphere here of old money and gentlemanly conduct, murmured business deals and colonial intrigue. It's the sort of place where you expect to encounter Alec Guinness and the titled cast of *Kind Hearts and Coronets*, or to overhear talk of naval intelligence and the Kaiser. The restaurant is splendidly wood-panelled, the reading room carries the London *Times* and the members' lockers are as likely to be filled with Havana cigars and Scotch whisky, as with sports gear.

Across the street from the Vancouver Club, there's another neo-Georgian facade. This is the Ceperley Rounsefell Company Building, completed in 1921 for a prominent insurance and real estate company. They commissioned English architects Sharp and Thompson, who reworked their Vancouver Club design on a smaller scale to produce this delicate offspring. The Georgian fanlight window, wrought-iron balcony, banded brickwork and harmonious composition are straight out of lithographs of London streets in the eighteenth century.

Ceperley Rounsefell & Building
One West Hastings St. Vancouver

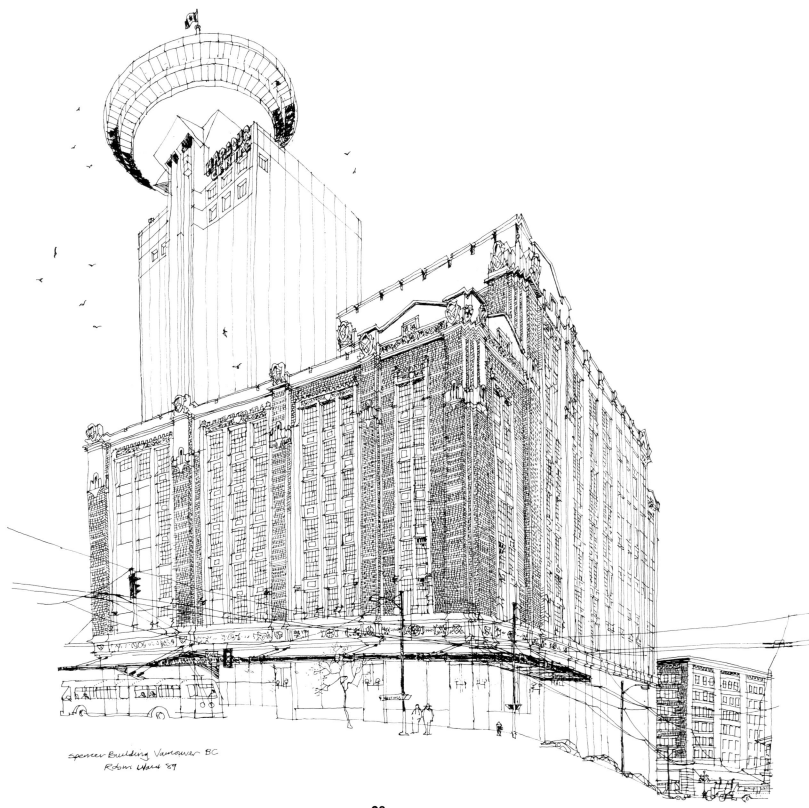

Spencer Building Vancouver BC
Robin Ward '89

Architects McCarter and Nairne designed this building, at West Hastings and Richards Streets, in 1928. Its soaring lines were a prelude to their Art Deco Marine Building (page 102) of 1930.

Originally the home of Spencer's Department Store, the building was remodelled in the mid-1970s when the adjacent Harbour Centre Tower was built. From a distance, the tower's revolving restaurant is an arresting skyline feature. From street level below, it looks like a flying saucer with sinister intentions, an unfriendly intruder on the Spencer Building's more traditional urban scale.

Architectural tradition has been re-established recently inside the old store. The first two floors have been redesigned as Simon Fraser University's downtown campus, in a style recalling the Vienna Secession of the early 1900s. This is a surprising, probably inadvertent, choice for a building with an Art Deco exterior but, for a university, it is a symbolic one. The architects of the Vienna Succession sought to come to terms with the modern world—a world from which Art Deco played truant.

David Spencer emigrated from Wales in 1862, setting up shop initially in Victoria, but expanding to Vancouver in 1906. Like Woodward's, Spencer's became a household name in Vancouver, remembered long after the store was sold to Eaton's in 1948. Several buildings comprised the department store, including the 1898 Italian palazzo-style Molson's Bank. Only the McCarter and Nairne building still stands today.

The three terra-cotta nurses that perched with sphinx-like poise high up on the Georgia Medical-Dental Building's corners were saved when the building was destroyed. Unfortunately for the preservationists, the potential quality of the new, postmodern building weakened arguments for retaining the old one. Postmodern buildings have frivolous tendencies: they are basically modern, but irrelevant historical details are stuck on for show. The new building, Cathedral Place, attempts to avoid this by referring to the local imagery around it. The new tower's chateauesque roof touches its hat to the Hotel Vancouver across Georgia Street, while the main block, ironically, is a replica of the Medical-Dental Building itself. But it's not old, and it's not Art Deco.

This structure, built in 1929, was designed by architects McCarter and Nairne. It was one of the city's few survivors of that era, a contemporary of the Marine Building (page 102) on Burrard Street (same architects, similar style) and, it was said, the latter's poor relation.

This argument was speciously used to justify dynamiting the building in 1989. While it didn't rank alongside the Marine Building in pure architectural terms, the Georgia Medical-Dental Building did have merit. Its contribution to the city's townscape was important and it had a mélange of attractive features, perhaps not noticed by people who went for dental treatment there. Like the Marine Building, it displayed curved and swirling Art Deco details and some beautifully crafted brickwork. The elaborate terra-cotta doorway had some runic panels showing medical and dental professions at work. The lobby contained a painted, beamed ceiling and a plaster frieze in neo-Mayan style. It could have been a film set for a bank robbery in Mexico City.

Georgia Medical-Dental Bldg.
Vancouver, Robin Ward 88

The Marine Building, Burrard St
Vancouver. Robin Ward '90

You could spend hours agog at this outstanding building's fabulous decor. In the two-storey, vaulted foyer, the light fittings are ships' prows breaking through the walls. The elevator doors are awash with bronze, bas-relief subsea flora while the cabs are panelled with Art Deco marquetry. In the 1930s, the lifts were operated by sailor-suited girls.

On the floor, originally linoleum, an astrological chart suggests voyages on predestined courses. Above the revolving doors, a full-rigged ship commemorating George Vancouver sails out of an Art Deco sunrise. Aquatic creatures abound. Outside, panels on the lower walls depict the transportation of the day: Zeppelins, dreadnoughts, biplanes and steam trains, all conceived with a febrile pen.

This is my favourite Vancouver view—the sudden panorama across the harbour from the foot of Burrard Street. Only from this angle is the Marine Building still pre-eminent, as it was when originally built.

When the Marine Building was opened in 1930, the architects claimed "...its architectural conception...suggests some great marine rock rising from the sea, clinging with sea flora and fauna, in sea green flashed with gold."

Architects McCarter and Nairne went overboard in applying symbolic decoration appropriate to Vancouver's emerging status as a port city of consequence and to a building that housed the principal grain, shipping, lumber, marine insurance and import-export merchants in the city. Terra-cotta friezes depicting Neptune and his creatures ripple across the facade like high-water marks. The doorway arch contains superb bas-relief panels illustrating the argosies of West Coast maritime history from Spanish galleons to CPR Empress liners. The foyer is a tour-de-force of 1930s decor, its vaulted doorway a cavernous threshold to an aquatic world.

Stylistically, European expressionist and futurist influences drifted ashore here on a high tide of classic North American Art Deco, coating the Marine Building with an international rather than purely provincial significance.

I'm tempted to open an account here so I can regularly go in and admire the decor: the period elevator lobby, balustraded stairway, Romanesque stonework, sphinx-like creatures on marble counters and the original bronze doors displayed downstairs. The main hall is flanked by Romanesque arches set on a floor plan with religious overtones. On the beamed ceiling, executed by Italian craftsmen, are illustrated homilies—"No Labour, no Bread," "Speed the Plough," "Success in the Fisheries"—a now quaint display of corporate paternalism. Outside choirs of round arches and medieval chevron mouldings rise to the top storeys.

When the Royal Bank commissioned this tower (begun in 1929 at Hastings and Granville Streets), they chose an architectural style that would send the appropriate message of solid, establishment respectability—not Art Deco (too frivolous), nor modernist (too adventurous), but twelfth-century Romanesque, with a touch of Florentine Renaissance.

The bank's chief architect, S. G. Davenport, had just supervised the completion of the Royal's Montreal headquarters, then the tallest building in the British Empire. His vision of this, the tallest and largest bank in Vancouver, was only half realized. Plans for the east wing of his skyscraping Tuscan palazzo were cancelled because of the Depression.

But enough remains of the original design to suggest just how grand the conception was. The building was patterned up twenty storeys with Romanesque stonework and crowned by a campanile. It boasted a stunning Florentine banking hall, derived from the even grander Montreal design. The Royal Bank, had it been completed, would have been the wonder of the west coast. It would have outshone even the contemporary, and today more celebrated, Marine Building (page 102). But even half-built, it is the more refined of the two—its finely cut stone, assembled with erudition and restraint, contrasts sharply with the Marine Building's flamboyant presence.

The Royal Bank Building, Vancouver
Robin Ward 1990

This building looks like something out of *Beau Geste*. English architect Adrian Gilbert Scott had planned a cathedral in Cairo in the 1930s, which explains the illusion of mud walls and Foreign Legion forts here.

There are rich, not to say bizarre, layers of architectural reference on this striking work. Scott belonged to the famous English architectural dynasty that specialized in Gothic Revival in the nineteenth century. There are some Gothic touches to the design—lancet windows, a squat, octagonal steeple, stylized gargoyles and, inside, wooden tracery.

Eastern Mediterranean influence also shows here. There is a minaret on the north wall and a Byzantine gloom and mystery in the arches, alcoves and hidden spaces inside. Yet the church is concrete and dates from 1937. The setbacks, parapets and entrance are boldly Moderne. Scott, who was probably expected by the clergy to have imitated an English village church, surprised them all with his daring design.

More conventional are the clergy house to the right of the church on Cordova Street, built in 1927 in Arts and Crafts style, and the 1925 parish hall on Gore Street, which looks like a manse in the Hebrides.

St James Anglican Church
Vancouver, Robin Ward 90

Vancouver's politicians turned down the Marine Building (page 102—what a town hall that would have made!) in favour of this purpose-built monument to local government. The Marine Building's developers, stung by the Wall Street crash, were looking for a buyer for their newly completed building at the time.

City Hall, at Cambie Street and West 12th Avenue, was completed in 1936, the 50th anniversary of the city's incorporation. A bas-relief above the main entrance, behind the statue of George Vancouver, commemorates this event by showing the new building and the tent of 1886 where council meetings were temporarily held after the great fire. Over the next fifty years, local government workers camped out in a series of Vancouver buildings, including the Tellier Tower (page 46), one reason why the city fathers were keen to have their own chambers.

Designed in 1930s Moderne style, a sort of Art Deco without the trimmings, City Hall now has an unmistakable period character. At the time it was built, it was absolutely up-to-date, a progressive symbol of an ambitious city, a building to be looked at with respect and admiration. Its symmetrical plan and gardens represented the imposition of order on the landscape, a metaphor for the order good government imposed on the city that this building overlooks.

City Hall is a bit pompous and self-important, in the way that politicians and bureaucrats can be, but in today's world of architectural lightweights, City Hall is refreshingly dignified.

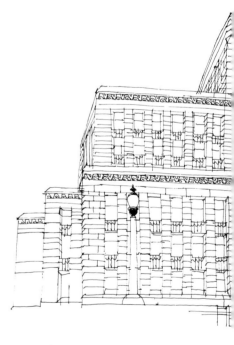

City Hall, Vancouver, Robin Ward 1990

"In anticipation of the Panama Canal opening, new trans-Pacific ships were calling, the completion of new railways was imminent . . . and federal grain commissioners were building Vancouver's first grain elevator." The Canadian government elevator of 1914 was the first built in Vancouver. By the early 1920s, the Port of Vancouver's trade had increased and several newer elevators were built. During the First World War, though, the original structure (at the foot of Woodland Drive) stood idle, earning its nickname, "Steven's Folly," after the local member of Parliament who had lobbied for its construction.

The engineers and architects who designed the great grain elevators built at most Canadian ports in the first half of this century didn't have great architecture in mind. You won't find any classical columns or surplus decoration on these buildings. The concrete structures, built to store prairie grain for export, were strictly utilitarian.

But look at how they're built! If you discovered them in the desert, you'd think they were mighty relics of some abandoned civilization. Grouped together, their sculptural ranks of concrete cylinders convey a silent, monumental dignity.

In the 1920s, European modernist architects, among them Le Corbusier no less, found a mythic quality in these concrete hulks—the sublimation of the "form follows function" credo of modern design. They seemed to personify the spartan Utopia of which progressive architects dreamed.

This is an interesting eddy of architectural history and a potential heritage argument, but it conceals a deeper truth. More than architectural theory, grain elevators honour all the anonymous tillers of the soil, the stoic prairie folk whose fortitude year after year still helps sustain our cushy urban way of life.

Grain Elevators, Vancouver
Robin Ward 1990

Owned by St. George's School, the former Convent of the Sacred Heart, at 29th and Wallace, has been a landmark on the West Side since it was built in 1912. Set in wooded grounds, it was built by the Sisters of the Sacred Heart, a teaching order founded in France in 1800 which established schools around the world. Like the Oblate Fathers, who built little Gothic churches wherever they went, the sisters chose Gothic Revival as the most suitable style to symbolize their mission to spread the word and enlighten their student charges.

Architecturally, the convent is of great interest. Its 300-foot-long granite facade, anchored by a massive Gothic port-cochère, is a strongly composed arrangement of pointed gables, battlemented parapets and bay windows. Above the port-cochère, the convent's name etched in Gothic script, the crest of the Sacred Heart, two gargoyles and a granite cross lend delicate detail to the muscular Christianity represented here.

The back of the building (also treated in Gothic but with an Arts and Crafts additional wing, now pleasantly ivy-covered like the adjacent Victorian-style gatehouse) is as interesting as the main facade. Irregularly patterned granite is featured but with a picturesque, rustic charm in contrast to the more academic Gothic stonework on the front. Galleries of Gothic ironwork overlooking an open courtyard recall the French colonial cast-iron balconies of Quebec City and New Orleans—again in contrast to the front which refers more to English 19th-century collegiate Gothic style.

Rich in architectural reference, the Convent of the Sacred Heart is an outstanding piece of British Columbia's architectural heritage.

Convent of the Sacred Heart
Vancouver, Robin Ward 1

Russian Orthodox Church
Vancouver, Robin Ward 89

Did I venture to Smolensk for this drawing? Well, not quite. No further than Strathcona, where this church stands incongruously on Campbell Avenue. Canada's immigrants bring more than their language and cuisine to this country. Here, the architecture came as well.

Churches of this type once sprouted on the prairies where, before the First World War, most Russian and Ukrainian immigrants settled. Although it was built in 1940, the Strathcona church was built in a style that can be traced back to twelfth-century Russia. In the tradition of these (usually rural) buildings, it was designed and built by the local priest, one Alexander Kiziun. He even added the customary onion domes, distinctive and practical features (snow falls away from them easily) that give the church its picturesque quality. Caught in occasional coastal snowfalls, it looks like a scene from *Dr. Zhivago*.

Strathcona, directly east of Chinatown, is the oldest residential settlement in Vancouver. Spreading south from Hastings Mill in a diaspora of shacks and frame houses, it was, in the 1880s, an egalitarian community where millworkers lived on the same streets as the mill owners.

By 1900, the well-to-do had moved to the more exclusive West End, leaving Strathcona the "jumble of mixed uses and patchwork of architectural styles" and mosaic of immigrant cultures that it remains today. With its modest houses, corner groceries, tumbledown lanes and salty air, it is still the small seaside town that it has always been.

When the Cathedral of Our Lady of the Holy Rosary was opened in 1900, it was pronounced "the finest piece of architecture west of Toronto and north of San Francisco"—more a leap of faith, I think, than an impartial judgement. Nevertheless, the church, with its twin spires, buttressed sandstone, vaulted ceiling, rose window and stained glass, is undeniably impressive.

Built at the corner of Dunsmuir and Richards on high ground—the site was chosen because the tallest tree in the city once stood here—the church once had an unobstructed view across Gastown to the North Shore mountains. Seen from the street, it stood alone on the skyline just as the medieval Gothic cathedrals of France, from which the Holy Rosary takes its sermon, were built to do. This historical connection is still apparent in the cathedral's form and style. Some irreverent zoning, though, has allowed a modern office tower to be built nearby.

As interesting as the cathedral is the saga of its bells. They were cast in France and shipped, as if on a medieval pilgrimage, via China and across the Pacific, only to be found to be out of tune. They were then sent to England to be recast and returned in 1906. Today, their happy clamour still rings out over the city.

The Holy Rosary Cathedral, Vancouver
Robin Ward 89

L'Eglise Saint Paul. Mission Indian Reserve, Vancouver
Robin Ward 89

"Home is the sailor, home from the sea." Long before the Lions Gate Bridge was built, l'Eglise Saint Paul was a landmark for ships approaching Vancouver harbour. It is still one of the most visible buildings on the North Shore.

The church was built in 1909, not for seamen but for the local Squamish Indians on whose Mission Reserve it still stands today. It's a poignant edifice, evoking the well-meaning, probably homesick French missionaries who built this miniature, medieval Gothic cathedral on a Pacific shore, and the disenfranchised natives for whose edification it was intended. There's still a rudimentary frontier feel here. The half-paved roads, scattered bungalows, telegraph poles and railway tracks to the interior seem to trap the church in its incongruous, colonial setting.

To an extent, I can envy the sense of purpose that impelled the nineteenth-century Oblate Fathers to build their Gothic churches far from home. But it is difficult to admire their (and others') denial of native culture. Canada's indigenous architecture may not have resembled European Gothic cathedrals, but the magnificent cedar houses built by the coastal tribes of British Columbia, particularly the Haida, were as spectacular in their setting and as symbolically important to the spiritual lives of the people.

Haida House UBC Museum of Anthropology, University Region Island 97

The Haida dwellings on the Queen Charlotte Islands reached their height of expression in the late nineteenth century. Some villages once boasted two dozen or more of these massive timber homes, each having its family of totem poles, rich with complex natural symbolism. Beginning in the late eighteenth century, European metal tools aided the elaboration of these works. But ultimately, outside influence destroyed many of the tribal societies.

Haida architecture is the main indigenous style in B.C., yet it seems to have had little influence on local buildings. The celebrated modern University of British Columbia Museum of Anthropology, outside which this reconstructed Haida house stands, is one of the few buildings in the province clearly inspired by native design.

This is a wee kirk with a weighty name. From the outside it looks small enough and has the appropriate look to be on a Christmas card—the sort with a cozy, snowbound, old English village scene.

It probably did look like this once, before being surrounded by the glossy towers of modern commerce, and it's not impossible to imagine the voices of the old church's pioneering congregation muffled by the snow of a nineteenth-century white Christmas.

Christ Church's significance is not measured by size but, in part, by the fact that it has survived. The building is over 100 years old, a centenary that seemed unlikely to enter the scriptures when the church was threatened with demolition in 1973. Its architectural merits were questioned at the time by those who saw only the unassuming exterior and the building's real estate value. Yet inside, a surprisingly spacious interior boasts some of the city's finest stained glass (you will find Captain Cook commemorated here) and a splendid, hammer-beamed cedar roof, all now protected by heritage designation.

Most of Vancouver's nineteenth-century buildings were framed with wood, the most symbolic of construction materials given British Columbia's essential logging industry. In Gastown, cedar pillars as impressive and thick as Greek columns support warehouse floors. Nowhere in the city, though, is the carpenter's art more masterfully expressed than inside Christ Church Cathedral.

Christ Church, Burrard and Georgia
Vancouver Robin Ward 1990

The Hotel Vancouver, West Georgia Street, Vancouver B.C.
Robin Ward 89

Canada has an architectural style all its own in the great Franco-Scottish chateauesque railway hotels built across the country since the late nineteenth century. These buildings are visible fragments of that elusive mosaic, the Canadian identity.

Almost every major Canadian city has one of these hotels, built by the Canadian Pacific, most of whose chiefs were Scottish, and Canadian National railways. The grande dame of them all was Le Chateau Frontenac, completed in Quebec City in 1893. The style followed the railways across the country. The buildings were designed to make well-to-do Europeans feel at home: the Banff Springs hotel was, according to William Cornelius Van Horne, the CPR's American general manager, to be "fit for a Highland Chieftain."

The Hotel Vancouver on West Georgia Street is one of the finest examples of this quintessentially Canadian building. Completed in 1939, it's an extraordinary structure, a mélange of gables and gargoyles, slightly Germanic in its moody, medieval romanticism but tempered by whimsical, symbolic details.

Above the Georgia Street entrance, a bas-relief illustrates a locomotive and an ocean liner steaming across the stonework, images from the days of soigné travellers. Hermes, their Greek guardian, head-dressed Indian chiefs, heraldic tableaux and a clan of carved chimera further animate the exterior. Inside, a Corinthian columned stairway, Rococo ballroom and assorted Art Deco motifs enhance the hotel's eclectic, eccentric decor.

Canadian Pacific have embarked on an ambitious and commendable restoration of their heritage hotels across the country. The success of this program can be seen particularly in Victoria, where Francis Rattenbury's Empress Hotel, built in 1908, has been polished to its former glory.

Rattenbury, the most prominent architect working in British Columbia at the time, also designed part of an earlier Hotel Vancouver and the city's Court House (page 22) in 1906.

Shaughnessy Heights was developed by the CPR on land granted to them as a reward for bringing the railway to Vancouver. Tree-lined streets and curving boulevards were laid out on the clear-cut land in the years before the First World War.

The oldest homes date from that time, and even those built later follow fashionable Edwardian styles—Mock Tudor, Queen Anne, Georgian Revival, English Arts and Crafts—lingering evidence of high society in an outpost of the British Empire.

Shaughnessy Heights is still an area of enviable prosperity and great architectural interest and variety. Many local architects gained commissions here, notably Samuel Maclure, the master of Mock Tudor, the most popular style because it symbolized the residents' origins and social aspirations. It also lent itself to local building materials and techniques. Against this Home Counties background, McRae's Italian villa is refreshingly continental.

"On a hill in Shaughnessy, overlooking the city and the mountains, an abandoned beauty languished, once the toast of Vancouver...Hycroft, gracious home of the McRae family had spent the war years as a veterans' hospital...deserted by the soldiers, it stood forlorn with peeling wall paper and echoing halls."

In 1961, the University Women's Club saw a potential home in those echoing halls. They bought the dilapidated mansion from the federal government, outbidding a developer who planned to pull the building down, thus saving the most splendid of all Shaughnessy homes.

The house was originally built for General Alexander Duncan McRae, whose fortune was made in lumber, mining, fisheries and real estate. In 1909, he chose to express his wealth in this Italianate mansion, designed by architect Thomas Hooper.

All the trappings of the Edwardian gentry were displayed here in thirty lavishly appointed rooms. Italian marble fireplaces, parquet floors, plastered ceilings, stained glass, fluted columns flanking a grand staircase and neoclassical landscape murals decorate the interior with studied affectation. Outside, a columned porte-cochère, like something out of *Gone With the Wind*, dominates the south facade, a device repeated on the north frontage overlooking the abundant foliage of a neoclassical garden. Even the stables (unfortunately demolished) featured a columned facade and oak floors for the McRaes' pampered ponies.

'Hycroft' McRae Avenue, Shaughnessy Heights
Vancouver, Robin Ward 1990

Stanley Park Tearoom, Vancouver
Robin Ward 1990

It's a tribute to the vision of Vancouver's Parks Board, and the watchful eye of citizens, that the natural beauty of Stanley Park has been preserved over the years. Of course, it's not all as wild as it seems. This is a subtly managed, cultivated wilderness, but still primitive enough that you can sense nature anxious to regain control.

There are few buildings in Stanley Park. This is not the Tuileries or St. James's, surrounded by public architecture and criss-crossed by imperial vistas. Stanley Park's formal embellishments have been left to gardeners rather than emperors and architects.

There was once a plan to build an Edwardian museum and art gallery at Lost Lagoon. The plan was revived in the 1920s as a speculative design in a style best described as "classical deco-cum-gothic revival." The structure would have been as large as City Hall and just as grand. But it would have been built in the wrong place.

The attraction of the buildings in the park is their vernacular, rather than urban, quality. The Stanley Park Pavilion, the tea room built in 1911 in the Swiss chalet style popularized by the CPR, is a good example. It looks handmade from the trees that once stood in its garden. There's a picturesque, amateurish charm here—all gables and rustic disorder. This building is completely at home in its wooded setting.

You can thank the Royal Navy and Royal Engineers for Stanley Park. In the 1850s, they surveyed the peninsula, intending to build artillery emplacements at Prospect Point to defend the narrows in the event of an American attack. Both Great Britain and the United States claimed disputed areas of the Pacific coast, a matter not entirely settled by the treaty of 1846 which established today's Canada/U.S. boundary.

By 1886, the need for a military reserve on the peninsula had diminished, and the city was allowed to annex the park from the Dominion government, thereby gaining an unrivalled amenity that remains one of Vancouver's most admired assets.

When the Sylvia Hotel was built in 1912, the West End was an elegant, leafy suburb of mansions and modest homes. Rezoning in the 1950s permitted the high-rise buildings that have completely changed the district.

The West End is still one of the most interesting parts of the city, though. The architectural free-for-all that resulted in the jumble of towers amidst surviving older buildings has given Vancouver its most lively and cosmopolitan residential community. You can hear as many languages on the streets as there are styles of architecture here.

Few of the modern buildings are of great merit individually, but collectively they make for a memorable skyline. At street level, the area's population density, one of the highest in Canada, gives the West End a distinctly European urban feel. The coastal light, when the climate isn't misbehaving, shimmers softly with a Mediterranean quality.

The Sylvia Hotel gives the impression that nearby Stanley Park is about to invade the city. In fact, the Virginia creeper that completely covers the main facade of this 1912 West End landmark was planted by one of the original lady residents of the Sylvia Court Apartments, as the hotel was first named. Like the old ladies who still populate the area, the building radiates the gentility of its years.

Winter is the best time of year to appreciate the Sylvia's architectural detail, which is otherwise obscured behind thick layers of foliage. The hotel is one of Vancouver's finer examples of Edwardian classicism and, until 1958, was the tallest building in the West End.

Having stayed here I can vouch for the Sylvia's old-fashioned character, not to say idiosyncrasies. When storms whistle in from the Pacific, the hotel, beached on English Bay, creaks like an old steamship, recalling a time when it was a landmark for mariners approaching Vancouver Harbour.

Also on English Bay, within sight of the Sylvia, is Alexandra Park, a delightful spot, given added period ambience by its picturesque cedar bandstand, constructed in 1914.

Alexandra Park Bandstand
Vancouver
Robin Ward 1990

the Sylvia Hotel, Vancouver
Robin Ward 1990

Barclay Manor, Barclay Street
Vancouver, Robin Ward 1990

Barclay Manor is one of the few old homes that still stand in the West End. It was built in 1904 for Frank Baynes, at the time the manager of the Dominion Hotel (which still stands in Gastown). Miss Clairmont's West End Hospital, a sanitarium with a genteel-sounding name, took over the house in 1909. By 1926 it had become Barclay Manor Boarding House, a fate that befell many West End mansions as their owners (those with the city's "old money") or the heirs sold up and moved to Shaughnessy Heights.

More recently, Barclay Manor has been restored as a social centre for the community's old people and is part of Barclay Square Heritage Park (1400 block Barclay Street). This unusual and attractive park was created by the city in the 1980s and it contains nine heritage homes built between 1890 and 1908.

The houses here, designed in eclectic Victorian style, show how the West End once looked. Some of them were designed in the Queen Anne style, which had its origin in early eighteenth-century England. Queen Anne was revived there in Victorian times as part of the general trend to the "picturesque"—a reaction to the rapid industrialization of the day.

Barclay Manor is one of the best surviving examples in Vancouver, displaying most of the characteristics of the style: an abundance of gingerbread gables, corbelled chimney, patterned (in this case diamond) shingles, shiplap siding, bay windows, stained glass and a sweeping, classically columned verandah.

The Queen Anne style was introduced to North America in 1876 at the Philadelphia Centennial Exposition, where the British government had built two houses in a half-timbered version of the style. The *American Builder* called them "most interesting." Others thought so, too: the style spread quickly across the continent.

The beauty of the Queen Anne style was its adaptability to local materials and individual tastes. Gables and cupolas, verandahs and chimneys could (and did) sprout everywhere. The houses had personalities as varied as their builders, from stuffy and formal to wildly eccentric. This diversity is shown to some extent by the contrast between Barclay Manor and the adjacent Roedde home (page 132).

The Roedde House was built in 1893 for Gustav Roedde, proprietor of Vancouver's first book bindery. Many houses built in Vancouver at this time were built either by the owners themselves or by local tradesmen or builders, who would usually copy architectural styles from picture books by which fashionable styles were circulated.

No style was more popular than Queen Anne. Gables, porches, turrets and ornamental woodwork could be assembled to satisfy individual whims rather than architects' rules. Few well-known architects worked on these vernacular dwellings, preferring larger and more lucrative commissions for mansions and country houses for the province's would-be aristocracy.

The Roedde House, however, has been attributed to none other than Francis Rattenbury, who was at the time working on his provincial Parliament Buildings design. At first glance, this seems an unlikely claim. The house is an attractive but unexceptional example of a style then commonplace across the continent, although the Jacobean turret is slightly unusual. Rattenbury adopted this picturesque accessory as part of his repertoire, and on the Roedde House there is a sure touch to the turret's form and detail. Rattenbury was working in Vancouver in 1892. He may not have designed the house but, fresh from England and with some experience, he may have been persuaded to let this little turret flow from his pen.

The Roedde House
Barclay Street, Vancouver
Robin Ward 1990

Kensington Place, Nicola Street, Vancouver
Robin Ward 89

Kensington, still a well-heeled part of London, was the inspiration, not to say aspiration, behind the name of this grandiose West End apartment building, built in 1914. At that time, British Columbia was still very British, as the names on many older buildings testify. West End apartment buildings include the Rothesay, the Beaconsfield, the Buckingham and others with names faithful to the crown.

But the Kensington's architect, one Philip M. Julien, wasn't thinking of the United Kingdom. The source of his inspiration was Italy. Built on Nicola Street at Beach Avenue, this house should have been called something like the Palazzo di Mare. Architecturally, we're on the shores of the Adriatic or Lake Garda here, rather than English Bay.

Julien's Italy, though, was either a dream or a faded memory. The design shows imagination rather than academic imitation, particularly in its decorative details. A multitude of ferocious lions' heads snarl from the cornice. The portico looks like a soufflé. Ornamental iron lamp standards strike a note of grandeur on the stairs and recessed balconies and adventurous use of concrete add a touch of originality to the theatrical Edwardian facade. Saved by the residents from threatened destruction some years ago, this, of all West End apartment buildings, is a Pavarotti among lesser voices.

The Banffshire was built at the corner of Melville and Jervis Streets just before the First World War. It's one of several large apartment buildings put up in the West End at that time, of which the Sylvia Hotel (page 128) is probably the best known example. Most of them still stand.

Like the Sylvia, many of these buildings were designed in an Italianate style as if for some street in Milan. Here, though, the style is neo-Georgian, with a hint of Jacobean. In London, many blocks of flats of this size and style can still be seen, dating mostly from the late nineteenth century.

Oriel windows (a bold feature here), patterned brickwork, Adamesque scrollwork, columned porticos and its Scottish name lend the Banffshire a convincing aura of fin-de-siècle, bourgeois society as exported to the British colonies.

Slightly shabby now, but retaining an air of distinction, the building has the demeanour of a retired colonial functionary of modest means. Given such a personality, the Banffshire might well be dismayed today, as encroaching highrise development and gentrification disturb its dozey, contented retirement.

Banffshire Apartments, Vancouver
Robin Ward 1990

The Pendera.
West Pender Street, Vancouver
Robin Ward 1990

The Pendera, designed for the Downtown Eastside Residents Association, is a building of special and unsung significance to this city. It's an exemplary model for inner-city housing and an alternative to the tall, isolated towers that characterize much contemporary residential development.

Located on Pender Street across from the Sun Tower (page 64), The Pendera is an instructive example of efficient high-density land use conforming to the existing street grid and urban fabric. This building fits in. Architecturally, it's a modest triumph. Eight storeys of recessed balconies refer cleverly to the nearby Chinatown tradition, and a strongly composed, brick-faced facade is both up-to-date and traditional, harmonizing with adjacent turn-of-the-century buildings. The combination gives the Pendera a timeless character. Was it built today or in 1910? It looks as if it's always been there.

In scale and appearance, the Pendera shares characteristics with the surviving nineteenth-century neighbourhoods of Paris, Vienna, Glasgow and other European cities, as well as those in Edwardian Vancouver. In those European cities, densely packed streets of four- to eight-storey apartment buildings, many of them with inner courtyards and ground-floor shops and small businesses, created vibrant mixed-use and mixed-income communities. They were built on a human scale, a practice that could be emulated here today.

There's something to be said for the nineteenth-century urban way of life to which the Pendera refers. In Canada, it gives Montreal its character and Victoria its charm. In Vancouver, the density of the West End where the buildings are not isolated but stand cheek-by-jowl, the vitality of Granville Island, the serendipity of Chinatown and the sympathetic restoration at the Sinclair Centre all play variations on this theme. These examples, along with the Pendera and others in the city, confidently and creatively adapt the proven patterns of the past to the needs of the present.

Overleaf: **Madrona Apartments** (1500 block West 15th Avenue), built in 1930, is one of many older apartment buildings that give the South Granville and West End neighbourhoods a notable urban unity and a fragile charm. Dating from the 1920s or earlier, they display delightful stylish quirks—Mock Tudor, bogus baronial, neoclassical and, at the Madrona, Spanish Colonial, which drifted north from California—a pot-pourri of architecural reference and the essential characteristic of Vancouver's architectural heritage.

'Madrona', W 15th Vancouver
Robin Ward '89

Adamesque: A style named after Robert Adam, the eighteenth-century Scottish architect and interior designer known for his refined, picturesque classicism.

Anthemion: Decoration found in Greek and Roman architecture and based on honeysuckle flowers and leaves, often applied as a continuous horizontal band.

Arcade: 1. A series of arches carried on columns or pillars, either free-standing or set in a wall. 2. A covered passage, traditionally with a glass roof, lined with shops on both sides.

Art Deco: A style fashionable between the wars, derived from the *Exposition des Arts Décoratifs* held in Paris in 1925. Its vivid Jazz Age imagery was most expressively applied to North American skyscrapers.

Art Nouveau: A European fin-de-siècle style characterized by free-flowing, plant-like forms and sinuous lines, often taken to bizarre extremes.

Arts and Crafts: A late nineteenth-century English style, not unrelated to Art Nouveau; generally anti-industrial with an emphasis on craftsmanship and traditional materials, and expressing pastoral values.

Baluster: A support for a railing, on stairs or a balcony; where extended, forming a balustrade.

Baronial: A social ambience rather than a style; quasi-medieval and Jacobean; popular with captains of industry and commerce in Victorian and Edwardian times.

Baroque: A seventeenth- and early eighteenth-century style of classical origin, curvaceous and often strongly composed and layered.

Bas-Relief: A sculptural or cast panel on which the figures or ornament are partially raised from the background.

Bay Window: An angular, projecting window, often three-sided; from BAY, the vertical division(s) on a facade.

Beaux-Arts: A style named fter the *École des Beaux-Arts*, the state art school in Paris and the premier architectural school in the late nineteenth century. The style was a luxurious, overblown classicism popular, particularly in North America, up until the 1920s.

Belle Epoque: The Edwardian era of gracious living, for those who could afford it, which ended with the First World War.

Belvedere: A small lookout tower; at ground level a gazebo.

Buttress: An angled stone, brick or timber support which gives the appearance of, and may actually be, holding up a wall.

Byzantine: The style of early medieval Christian architecture, in southern central Europe and later in Russia, characterized by flat domes and dark, enigmatic interiors.

Campanile: The Italian term for a bell tower, either separate from or part of the main building. More generally used to describe any tower in Italianate style.

Capital: The uppermost feature on a column or pilaster, either plain or decorated. In classical architecture, there are four main styles of capitals/columns: Doric, Ionic, Corinthian and Tuscan.

Cartouche: An ornamental panel in the form of a scroll, sometimes with an inscription and often elaborately framed.

Caryatid: A sculpted figure, often life size or larger, usually female, supporting an entablature.

Cast Iron: Commonly used in the nineteenth century, in place of stone or timber for columns and decorative features. In some cases complete facades were assembled in cast iron.

Chateauesque: An elaborate style derived from sixteenth-century French chateaux. Popular in the late nineteenth century, it then included Scottish baronial and Gothic features blended with the original classicism. It is the classic Canadian architectural style.

Cherub: A chubby, childlike figure, often winged, in Renaissance art.

Chevron: A medieval, V-shaped pattern in Romanesque architecture; also an Art Deco feature.

Classicism: The architecture of ancient Greece and Rome from whose principles of form and composition most non-Gothic Western architecture is derived; frequently revived and adapted throughout the centuries.

Clerestory Window: The upper window of a building, if treated separately from the main facade, providing high light to the interior.

Colonnade: A procession of columns carrying arches or an entablature.

Corinthian: The most ornate classical order, distinguished by foliated capitals.

Corbel: A bracket or block projecting from a wall and supporting, often in series, a cornice, balcony or other horizontal feature.

Cornice: The projecting, normally topmost, horizontal feature on a building, usually running the full width of the facade.

Cupola: A small dome crowning a roof or other feature; circular or many-sided.

Dado: The waist-high finish applied to an interior wall, traditionally tiled or wood-panelled; originally part of a classical pedestal.

Dome: A major feature, usually hemispherical, on a large building.

Doric: The oldest classical order, with heavy, fluted columns and plain capitals.

Eaves Gallery: A row of small columns framing clerestory windows directly below a cornice.

Entablature: In classical architecture, the horizontal beam, often extended, spanning and supported by columns.

Expressionism: An angst-ridden, early twentieth-century northern European style related to Art Nouveau, characterized by exaggerated angles and often executed in imaginative brickwork.

Facade: The front of a building and the canvas for any architectural expression.

Fanlight: A radiating window, usually above a door, in Georgian architecture.

Fluting: Repeated concave grooves running vertically up a column or pilaster, usually on Doric order.

Fretwork: A band of geometric, maze-like ornament in Greek and Chinese architecture.

Frieze: 1. A decorative or plain band on an entablature. 2. Any wide, decorative band along a wall, particularly below a cornice.

Futurism: An anarchic Italian movement, c. 1914, which glorified technology, modern architecture and transport.

Gable: The wall segment, or complete wall, punctuating the end of a pitched roof, usually triangular in elevation.

Galleria: An Italian arcade or any arcade, particularly a grand one, with galleries on more than one level. Also a term used to dignify a shopping mall.

Gargoyle: Traditionally a water spout projecting from a roof parapet, carved as a grotesque animal or human figure.

Garland: A carved or moulded hanging arrangement of fruit or leaves set in a panel; also known as a festoon.

Georgian: A subtle classicism in eighteenth- and early nineteenth-century Britain.

Gingerbread: Fanciful, carved woodwork applied to gables and porches, particularly on Victorian homes; named after the icing decorating German cakes.

Gothic: Architecture characterized by pointed, as opposed to curved, arches. With classicism, the main influence on Western architecture, but revived periodically rather than frequently; more northern than southern European and with definite religious and medieval overtones.

Hacienda: In Spain, a large estate or house; broadly classical with overhanging tile roofs.

Historicism: A nineteenth-century term, not necessarily flattering, describing the contemporary revival of past architectural styles.

Ionic: A classical order, the capital of which is composed of two or four spiral scrolls.

Italianate: Generally a nineteenth-century style of picturesque classicism with broad overhangs and round-arched windows.

Jacobean: An early seventeenth-century style in Britain identified by heavily mullioned windows, Flemish gables, heavy wood-panelled interiors and flattened cupolas.

Lancet Window: A narrow, pointed, arched window found on Gothic designs.
Lantern: A small turret or cupola with windows on all sides, surmounting a dome.
Low-Tech: A modern vernacular style using basic, easily manufactured materials.

Marquetry: Woodwork employing multi-coloured inlay, highly finished; often found in Art Deco interiors of buildings and ocean liners of the period.
Minaret: A tall, slender tower on a mosque.
Mock Tudor: The style of Tudor England as revived in the nineteenth and twentieth centuries, notably on houses with country manor pretensions: brick chimneys, half-timbered walls with white stucco infill and steeply pitched roofs.
Moderne: A soft, streamlined modernism or Art Deco without the decoration.
Modernism: The architecture of the mid-twentieth century. Often called the "International Style"; a sometimes dogmatically applied, bare-bones style of concrete, steel and glass, in which its proponents' "form follows function" precept outlawed decoration.
Moulding: The pattern on a projecting band on a facade or interior wall, often continuous.

Mullion: Vertical unit dividing glazed areas in a window.

Neoclassicism: A general term for any classical revival.

Oriel Window: A bay window projecting from above ground floor level; often continuing up a facade and repeated in each bay.
Order: In classical architecture, the structural component comprising columns and entablature. The five classical "orders," each a variation on the theme, are Doric, Ionic, Corinthian, Tuscan and Composite.

Palazzo: Italian palace, mansion or ornate block of flats; particularly the large urban dwellings built by fifteenth-century Florentine merchant dynasties.
Palladian: A style named after Andrea Palladio, the sixteenth-century Italian architect famed for his intellectual classicism.
Palmette: A fan-shaped ornament in the form of a palm leaf.
Parquet: Hardwood flooring laid in a repeat pattern of small, thin pieces.
Pediment: The triangular section above a portico or window; often containing sculptural groups, and sometimes curved or "broken," that is, with the upper or lower centre removed.
Pilaster: A rectangular column, projecting slightly from a wall, usually con-

forming to a classical order.
Porte-Cochère: A pillared or columned canopy outside a main entrance, originally designed for horse-and-carriage shelter.
Portico: A large, columned entrance porch, open or partly enclosed, normally classical in style.
Postmodernism: A 1970s stylistic reassessment of Modernism, originally serious-minded, but now unashamedly commercial and frivolous; characterized by a debased and meaningless historicism.

Queen Anne: A popular late Victorian/Edwardian residential style, noted for its whimsical use of gables, porches, picturesque roof lines and gingerbread.

Renaissance: In Italian, the *rinascimento* or rebirth of classical art and architecture in fifteenth-century Florence and then elsewhere in Europe.
Return: The part of a building, or detail thereof, that is carried back at right angles from the facade; for example, partially down a lane or into a doorway.
Rococo: A delicate, late baroque style applied to interior design rather than architecture.
Romanesque: The round-arched, medieval style that preceded and influenced Gothic and Renaissance design.
Rose Window: A circular window, usually on a church, with segmented trac-

ery arranged like the petals on a flower.

Rotunda: 1. A building with a circular plan, usually domed and occasionally enclosed by a colonnade. 2. A circular room or staircase, also domed; especially in Palladian architecture.

Rusticated: Roughened for a rustic effect; usually refers to stonework composed of heavy blocks roughly chipped on the exposed side, giving a deep texture to facades, usually on the ground floor.

Scrollwork: Ornament in the form of parchment partly unrolled or a lightly inscribed flourish or motif.

Second Empire: The style of mid-nineteenth-century France, especially Paris, up until 1870; a pompous neoclassicism marked by ostentatious detail and capacious mansard roofs.

Sino-Portuguese: A colonial style in Southeast Asia, which applied classical features to the upper floors of two-storey Chinese shop-houses.

Steel Frame: A construction technique developed in the late nineteeth century which, with the invention of the elevator, led to skyscraper design.

Terra-Cotta: Fired clay and sand, easily moulded to produce complex patterns and ornament, sometimes with a glazed finish. A popular substitute for stone in the nineteenth century and on early twentieth-century skyscrapers.

Tracery: Interlacing on the upper part of a panel, screen or window; usually Gothic and occasionally applied to ceilings.

Vaulted: A ceiling or roof arched in a semi-circular, pointed or other fashion.

Vienna Secession: A style developed by a group of artists and architects in fin-de-siècle Vienna who rebelled against the historicism of the late Victorian era.

Wrought Iron: Iron hand-beaten into the desired form. In appearance, wrought iron's thin strips and flakes are lighter and more delicate than the uniform finish of cast iron, with which it is often confused.

The drawings in this book were sketched outdoors, freehand, in ink, using a 0.2 Rapidograph technical pen. The originals, each of which can take several hours or up to a week to complete, are larger than they appear on these pages—in most cases drawn on 12x16'' or 18x24'' Canson and Strathmore sketchbooks.

The quotations in this book are taken from the following published sources:

Page 8 *Vancouver's First Century* (City of Vancouver 1977), *Greater Vancouver Illustrated* (Dominion Illustrating Co. 1908) **11** *Moderne Architektur* (Anton Schroll & Co. 1907, Getty Centre 1988); *Edinburgh, Picturesque Notes* (Seeley & Co. 1895) **25** *Le Temps des Gares* (Centre Pompidou 1978) **26–27** Canadian Pacific Staff Bulletin (Nov-Dec 1948) **30** From ''Sea Fever'' by John Masefield (1878–1967) **33/36** *Vancouver's First Century* **54** *A Walking Tour Through History* (City of Vancouver Planning Department 1987) **61** *Vancouver, the Golden Years 1900–1910* (Vancouver Museum 1971) **111** *Vancouver, an Illustrated History* (Lorimer 1980) **115** *A Walking Tour Through History* **116** Holy Rosary Cathedral Guide **119** From the Epitaph by Robert Louis Stevenson (1850–1894) **124** *A History of the University Women's Club of Vancouver* (1982)

With special thanks to my wife Porta, to the staff of the Vancouver Sun, where most of these drawings first appeared, to the many people who encouraged me to compile this book, and to those who helped produce it.